FENCING

A RENAISSANCE TREATISE

৶৶

Portrait of Camillo Agrippa.

Fencing

A Renaissance Treatise

by

Camillo Agrippa

ᔕᕒᕽ

Translated and
with an Introduction by
Ken Mondschein

Italica Press
New York
2009

ITALICA PRESS, INC.
595 Main Street, Suite 605
New York, New York 10044

Library of Congress Cataloging-in-Publication Data
Agrippa, Camillo, d. 1595?
  [Trattato di scientia d'arme. English]
  Fencing : a Renaissance treatise / by Camillo Agrippa ; translated and with an
introduction by Ken Mondschein.
    p. cm.
  Includes bibliographical references.
  Summary: "Agrippa's Treatise, first published in 1553, is considered a fundamen-
tal text of Western swordsmanship. It examines the art, reduces it to its principles,
and reconstructs it according to concepts of art, science and philosophy.
Introduction, glossary, notes, appendix, bibliography, 67 original illustrations"--
Provided by publisher.
  ISBN 978-1-59910-129-3 (pbk. : alk. paper) -- ISBN 978-1-59910-150-7
(e-book)
  1. Fencing--Early works to 1800. 2. Swordplay--Early works to 1800. I.
Mondschein, Ken. II. Title.
  U860.A3 2009
  796.86--dc22
                                                                        2009027095
Cover: The Third Guard from Camilla Agrippa's *Trattato di scientia d'arme.*

For a Complete List of
Italica Medieval & Renaissance Texts
Visit Our Web Site at
www.italicapress.com

To Aunt Arlene, in Loving Memory

CONTENTS

LIST OF ILLUSTRATIONS

Plates listed in italics *are not part of the original treatise, but have been added by the translator as notes or to aid intelligibility.*

ACKNOWLEDGEMENTS

First and foremost, I must gratefully acknowledge the generous contribution of Malcolm Fare, editor of *The Sword*, who laboriously photographed and e-mailed the images from his famous copy of Agrippa to me. Without him, this book would no doubt be illustrated by crude Microsoft Paint renditions of Agrippa's beautiful copperplate engravings.

No less a thank-you must go to Ramon Martinez and Jeannette Acosta-Martinez, to whom I owe the majority of my knowledge of fencing.

To Richard Gyug of Fordham University, my heartfelt thanks for revising my initial translation with me over the course of the spring 2006 semester, and for tolerating my insistence on reading Annibale's parts in the voice of Peter Lorre.

To Donald La Rocca, Richard Gradkowski, and the staff of the Arms and Armor Department of the Metropolitan Museum of Art for allowing me access to the collection, for sharing their knowledge, and for many interesting conversations in the employee cafeteria.

To Sydney Anglo and his wife Margaret McGowan, I am grateful for not only bringing serious academic consideration to the fencing treatise as a historical document, but also for learned commentary on my initial forays into getting a grip on Agrippa.

To my partner Amanda Kirk, for all her help, editing, encouragement, proofreading, and eating my cooking.

To William Wilson, for scanning, hosting, and placing a PDF copy of Agrippa's treatise in the public domain. Having a copy of Agrippa available for reference on my laptop was a vast improvement over laboriously copying the text in the bowels of special-collection rooms.

To no small number of friends and teachers for their help and encouragement: Keith Alderson, Charles Carman, Bob Charron, Phil Crawley, Puck and Mary Curtis, Jeffrey Forgeng, Matt Galas, Tom Glick, Sean Hayes, Steve Hick, Kenneth Hodges, William H.

Leckie, Jr., Arthur Kinney, Jared Kirby, Maryanne Kowaleski, Devon Kurtz, Jeff Lord, Andrea Lupo-Sinclair, Cai Marshall, Marie-Anne Michaux, Mark Millman, Steve Muhlberger, Roger Rouland, Sylvain Piron, Steven Reich, Roger Siggs, Paul Sise, Dan Smail, Charles Stinger, and Amy West.

Finally, to Patri Pugliese, without whom the Western Martial Arts Renaissance would have never happened.

ৰ৻৶

PREFACE

This is the first complete English translation of Camillo Agrippa's 1553 Treatise on the Science of Arms *(Trattato di Scientia d'Arme)*, a book that has not been reprinted in any language in over four hundred years. Best known as the first work on the rapier, the weapon that was the constant companion of the early modern gentleman, Agrippa's treatise uses the idiom of sixteenth-century humanism to both argue against earlier ideas about fencing and to set out the fundamental principles that all later theorists of fencing incorporated and reacted to.

This translation from the Italian is taken from the 1553 first printing and presented together with reproductions of its original copperplate engravings, with notes, a bibliography, glossary, and introductory material intended both to make this material accessible to the non-fencer or scholar unfamiliar with this genre of source material and to explicate Agrippa's milieu as a member of the circle that formed around the famed patron and antiquarian Cardinal Alessandro Farnese.

As a man of letters living in sixteenth-century Rome, Agrippa sought to incorporate into his work newly fashionable ideas about the universe and humanity's place within it. His treatise is thus a document of early modern concepts of the body, ideas about the social use of violence and conflict-resolution, and the ways in which conflict between social groups gave rise to new religious and cultural symbols that, in turn, helped to form proto-Enlightenment thought.

This translation will thus be of great interest not only to fencers and those interested in the history of fencing, but also to art historians, intellectual and cultural historians, students of the history of science and hermetic thought, and those studying constructions of masculinity and honor in early modern Italy.

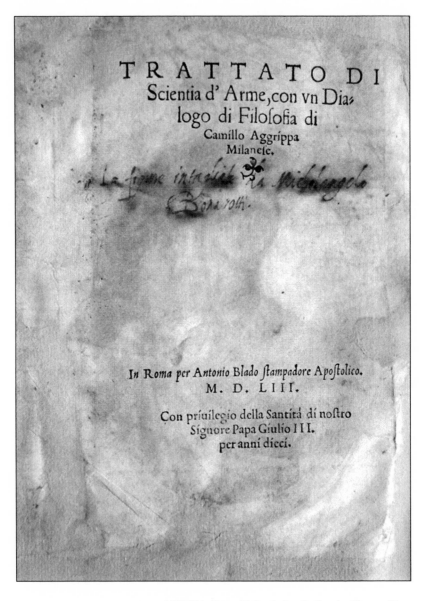

TRATTATO DI
Scientia d' Arme, con vn Dia‑
logo di Filosofia di
Camillo Aggrippa
Milanese.

La figure intagliate di Michelangelo Bonaroti.

In Roma per Antonio Blado stampadore Apostolico.
M. D. LIII.

Con priuilegio della Santità di nostro
Signore Papa Giulio III.
per anni dieci.

1553 Title Page with Inscription Attributed to Torquato Tasso.

INTRODUCTION

"...[Agrippa's] book is original, and much in advance of the popular
notions of his days."
— Egerton Castle, *Schools and Masters of Fence* (1885)

"Naturally, you must expect me to attack with Capo Ferro — "
"Naturally...but I find Thibault cancels out Capo Ferro, don't you?"
"Unless the enemy has studied his Agrippa — which I have!"
— Dialogue from Inigo Montoya's (Mandy Patinkin) duel with
Wesley/The Man in Black (Cary Elwes) in the 1987 cinematic
adaption of William Goldman's *The Princess Bride*

Early modern treatises on fencing and other martial arts, dealing
as they do with a subject that was such a key part of the early
modern elite male *habitus*, represent a almost-untapped wellspring
of insights that should be examined by modern scholars with the
utmost seriousness. To be sure, though, one who would assault such
texts must be armed not only with an understanding of history, but
also a technical knowledge of the subject. For one outfitted with
this panoply, such works as Camillo Agrippa's *Trattato di Scientia
d'Arme* are well worthy of serious study.

Agrippa's widely influential treatise represents not only a
turning point in the history of fencing, but also a microcosm of
sixteenth-century thought. Contained within this slim volume
are concrete examples of the questioning of received wisdom and
the turn to empirical proof that are considered the hallmarks of
the Enlightenment, evidence for a redefinition of elite masculinity
in the wake of the military revolution of the sixteenth century,
suggestions as to the place of the hermetic tradition in the early
modern intellectual milieu and its implications for the origins of
modern science, and — on a deeper level — arguments for the
transhistorical nature of certain human universals that provide
a powerful challenge to current fashions in the reading of texts.
The paradigm shift represented in Agrippa's *Trattato* reflects the
larger changes taking place in the early modern world: the incep-
tion of the modern nation-state, the print and military revolu-
tions, the rise of the self-fashioned man, and the increasingly

sophisticated use of number to explain the principles underpinning the tangible world.

Agrippa, being an amateur and not a professional teacher of arms — he was, in fact, an engineer by trade — was able to conceive of a radical re-imagining of the pedagogy of the art of fencing. To use his own term, it is a *ragionaménto*, that is, a reasoning or discourse that examines the art, reduces it to its very principles, and reconstructs it according to his own way of thinking — a way of thinking that incorporated new concepts of art, science, and philosophy.[1] In contrast, the author of the previous generation's most acclaimed and well-known work, the Bolognese master Achille Marozzo, seems almost locked into the mindset of a medieval guild or confraternity.[2] In Marozzo's *Opera nova*, published in Modena in 1536,[3] to learn to fence was to be initiated into a *mestiero*, that is to say a craft-guild, involving oaths to God, his mother, and the Cavalier St. George.[4] This mindset marked Marozzo's pedagogy, which he had learned from his master, Guid'Antonio di Luca (died c. 1514), and which di Luca in turn had likely learned from Filippo di Bartolomeo Dardi (died c.

---

1.   C.f. Florio's *New World of Words* (London, 1611) p. 419, col. 1, where he defines *ragionáre* as "to reason, to discourse, to speak, to talk, to parlie" and *ragionáto* as "reasoned, discoursed, talked, spoken. Also used for regular or conformable unto reason and judgment."

2.   Marozzo was preceded in print in the fifteenth century by the Spanish masters Jaime Pons (1474) and Pedro de la Torre, whose works, unfortunately, do not survive, by Pietro Monte's *Exercitiorum atque artis militaris collectanea* (Milan, 1509), and by Marozzo's fellow Bolognese Antonio Manciolino, also of a similar mentality, who seems to have published a work also entitled *Opera nova* in perhaps 1509. Our knowledge of Pons and de la Torre is from Luis Pacheco de Narvaez' 1672 *Nueva ciencia y filosofia de la destreza de las armas*; on Monte, see Sydney Anglo, "The Man Who Taught Leonardo Darts: Pietro Monti [sic] and His 'Lost' Fencing Book," *The Antiquaries Journal* 59.2 (1989): 261–78. Only copies of the 1531 reprinting of Manciolino are known and were obscure to fencing historians until relatively recently.

3.   Thimm, in his *Complete Bibliography of Fencing and Dueling* (New York: Bloom, 1890) erroneously gives a date of 1517.

4.   Marozzo, *Opera nova*, chap. 1.

1464), who began to teach fencing about 1413 and afterwards became in addition a professor of arithmetic and geometry at the University of Bologna.[5]

There may have been a long-standing connection between geometry, mathematics, and Marozzo's tradition of swordsmanship, but there is little in his work that appears mathematical to the modern mind. Like a medieval memory-palace brought to life, Marozzo's students run through a series of postures with colorful mnemonic names, such as the "guard of the long and extended tail," "head guard," "face guard," and "iron door guard of the boar," being instructed on the use of each for offense and defense. While we can assume this was an effective pedagogy — it was, after all, a school that was already at least a hundred years old, and Marozzo's book, as well as works espousing systems akin to his own, continued to be reprinted into the seventeenth century — it was also a very *medieval* mindset.[6] Whereas we can imagine Marozzo's student as the son of a prosperous, but fundamentally conservative, Italian burgher, Agrippa's reader–cum–disciple, like the author himself, is the self-fashioned man of the mid-sixteenth century. And, while Agrippa was on the cutting edge, as it were, of intellectual

---

5.   See Francesco Novati's notes to *Flos duellatorum* (Bergamo: Istituto Italiano d'Arti Grafiche, 1902), p. 108, n. 179; E. Orioli's article in *Il Resto del Carlino*, 20–21 maggio 1901 a. XVIII, n. 140; and Guido Pantanelli, "Scherma e maestri di scherma Bolognesi [sic]," in *Strenna storica Bolognese* 3 (1930): 45–49. My gratitude to Steve Hick and Matt Galas for referring me to these sources.

6.   Marozzo's second printing was Bologna, 1546; the third, Venice, 1550; the fourth, Venice, 1568; the fifth, Verona, 1615. Some hold, based on the similarities between the systems described by Manciolino, Marozzo, Viggiani's *Lo schermo* (written 1550, published in Venice in 1575), Agocchie's *Dell'arte di scrimia* (Venice, 1572), and the "Anonimo Bolognese" (MS Ravenna M-345 and M-346, ed. by Marco Rubboli and Luca Cesari as *L'Arte della spada* (Rimini: Il Cerchio, 2005) that there was a continuing Dardi "school." Though there are definite similarities that let us speak of a Bolognese "style," in the absence of definitive testimony, the existence of a distinct Dardi lineage has not been conclusively proven to my satisfaction.

fashion, his innovations have had lasting value — as is proven by the fact that the ideas he introduced have formed the foundation for fencing theory and pedagogy until the present day. We must bear in mind that his work has had enduring value precisely because the principles he expressed were found, by hard experience, to be efficacious when lives were on the line.

In short, Agrippa's *Treatise on the Science of Arms* is an explanation of a very practical system for handling a sword, expressed in the idiom of a sixteenth-century intellectual. It is this cultural enmeshment that has simultaneously led to the misunderstanding of Agrippa's work up to this point and that makes him such a rich source for understanding a critical moment in the development of Western thought.

Agrippa the Man

Given Agrippa's lasting fame (at least in fencing circles), we know shockingly little about his life. Even his name is most likely an invention, intended to recall the Roman general and architectural patron, and perhaps the magical theorist Henry Cornelius Agrippa of Nettersham. What we can be sure of, however, is that he was a man tied up in a network of politics and patronage. Agrippa's interlocutor in the dialogue that forms the last part of the *Trattato* is Annibale Caro (1507–66), a playwright best known for his metrical Italian translation of the *Aeneid* (published posthumously in 1581). Caro had worked his way up from being the private tutor to the wealthy of Florence to serving as a private secretary to Pietro Ludovico Farnese, duke of the papal fief of Parma, and, after the latter's 1547 assassination, to his three sons, Ottavio (who succeeded Pietro as duke) and the cardinals Ranuccio and Alessandro, before he achieved some measure of financial security through ecclesiastical benefices and his own literary efforts.[7]

---

7. Caro is also recorded as being one of the members of Cardinal Alessandro's household in 1554. See Fernand Benoit, "La Maison du cardinal Farnése en 1554," *Mélanges d'archéologie et d'histoire* 40 (1923): 198–206.

Caro is also famous for his feud with Lodovico Castelvetro, which began in 1553 after the latter criticized a sonnet the former had written in praise of the ruling French Valois family. It ended when Caro's denunciations of Castelvetro to the Inquisition and resulted in the latter's confinement in 1560, and according to Caro, in the 1555 murder of his friend Alberigo Longo. This was more than the mere squabbling of writers, but was embedded in a larger political conflict: Caro's patron Duke Pietro was the illegitimate son of Alessandro Farnese, who sat on St. Peter's throne from 1534–49 as Paul III and who was succeeded in 1550 by Julius III (who died in 1555). Julius' long, acrimoniously contested election was the result of anti-French collusion between the representatives of the emperor, Charles V, and the Farnese faction; in return for his support, the new pope confirmed Ottavio in his fief as duke of Parma, which had passed to a papal legate following his father's assassination. However, Emperor Charles decided it was more to his advantage to back Ferrante Gonzaga in his bid to retain the former Farnese territory of Piacenza and even take over Parma itself, and so the Farnese were compelled to shift alliances. They accordingly aligned with the French against the emperor, and in retribution Julius moved to deprive them of Parma. The French, however, triumphed militarily and Ottavio came to a separate arrangement with Charles (who was, helpfully, a former military ally of his, as well as the father of his wife, Margaret, later regent of the Netherlands). By 1552 Julius, defeated politically, had retired to the luxurious Villa Giulia, where he spent his time raising handsome adolescents to the office of cardinal, admiring his homoerotic frescos of putti, and intermittently supporting the Jesuits.[8] The factional rift, however, remained — and with literary criticism carrying stakes such as these, we can easily see why Agrippa's art was of practical interest to sixteenth-century men of letters.

---

8.   For a more detailed account of the political milieu, see John Goldsmith Phillips and Olga Raggio's "Ottavio Farnese" in *The Metropolitan Museum of Art Bulletin*, New Series 12.8 (Apr. 1954): 233-40.

The depopulated medieval city of Rome, with its malarial marshes and Forum turned to cow pasture was, in Agrippa's time, attracting new sorts of pilgrims — craftsmen, courtiers, artists, and intellectuals drawn to the splendor and patronage of the resurgent Renaissance papacy.[9] From the context of his work, Agrippa is clearly Caro's client: as has been the custom since the days of ancient Rome, it is the former's duty to call on the latter in his home. Agrippa, no doubt, would have liked to have replicated his friend's rise, and it is the perspective of the man of talent born outside of the traditional networks of power, but eager for the patronage of the great, that informs Agrippa's work.[10] The continual cycle of patron and poverty familiar to us from Cellini's memoirs would have been familiar to Agrippa.

The *Trattato* is dedicated to Cosimo I de' Medici, duke of Florence (if not yet of all of Tuscany), who, interestingly enough, also depended on Charles V for support.[11] Other of Agrippa's friends whom he name-drops in the dialog include Alessandro Corvino, friend of Pietro Aretino, and Titian who was well-known as a man about town and whose 1562 will states that the renowned collector, scholar, patron, and politician Cardinal Alessandro Farnese (that is, the son of the assassinated duke and grandson of Paul III) was in debt to him for 1,000 *scudi* for the purchase of

---

9.   See on this Charles Stinger, *The Renaissance in Rome* (Bloomington: Indiana University Press, 1985), 28–29.

10.   For a more extensive discussion of this spoils system, see Gigliola Fragnito's article on "Cardinals' Courts in Sixteenth-Century Rome," *The Journal of Modern History* 65 (Mar. 1993): 26–56.

11.   Why the treatise is dedicated to Cosimo instead of Alessando Farnese is unclear to me; however, some possible theories are offered below.

antiquities[12]; the artist Francesco Siciliano[13]; the writer and anti-quarian Hieronimo (better known as "Gerolamo") Garimberto, bishop of Gallese; Alessandro Ruffino, scion of that famous family; Alessandro Cesati, called Greco, a scholar of Greek, well-known medallist, head of the papal mint, and familiar of the cardinal[14]; and the Mannerist painter Francesco Salviati, who had also worked for Cardinal Farnese (for instance, on his private chapel in the Cancelleria)[15] and who is well-known for his use of *contrapposto* positions derived from the Belvedere Torso.[16] The "Ph. [Phillip] Salutiarum" of the *motu propio* is no doubt Fillipo Archinto, archbishop of Saluzzo (Latin *Salutiensis*), who was appointed vicar-general of Rome by Paul III and whose portrait by Titian today hangs in the Metropolitan Museum of Art. Farnese allegiance, in particular membership in the artistic circle and even the household of Cardinal Alessandro Farnese, was one common feature of this group; another was the devotion to antiquity that marks both the cardinal's circle and Agrippa's work. One final figure mentioned by Agrippa, Iacomo del Negro, remains obscure.

---

12.   Thomas Ashby, "The Bodelian MS. of Piro Ligorio," *The Journal of Roman Studies* 9 (1919): 181–82. Corvino is also the addressee of Aretino's famous letter decrying Michelangelo's *Last Judgment*. See Erica Tietze-Conrat, "Neglected Contemporary Sources Relating to Michelangelo and Titian," *The Art Bulletin* 25.2 (June 1943): 155.

13.   Siciliano is obscure but is mentioned in Filippo Titi's *Descrizione delle pitture, sculture e architetture esposte in Roma* (Rome: Marco Pagliarini, 1674), 159, 340.

14.   Benoit, 201.

15.   On this and for a brief biography of the cardinal, see Patricia Rubin, "The Private Chapel of Cardinal Alessandro Farnese in the Cancelleria, Rome," *Journal of the Warburg and Courtauld Institutes* 50 (1987): 82–112. The standard sources on the Farnese and Alessandro are, respectively, Giovanna R. Solari and Frederic Tuten, *The House of Farnese* (Garden City, NY: Doubleday, 1968); and Clare Robertson, "Il Gran Cardinale": *Alessandro Farnese, Patron of the Arts* (New Haven: Yale University Press 1992).

16.   For instance, in his *Decollation of the Baptist*. See David Summers' "*Contrapposto*: Style and Meaning in Renaissance Art," *The Art Bulletin* 59.3 (Sept. 1977): 336–61.

As the title page of his *Trattato* indicates, Agrippa identifies himself as Milanese, but according to his own account he arrived in Rome on the 26th of October 1535, where he set to work discussing with the architect Antonio Sangallo the Younger and Michelangelo Buonarroti (both of whom had worked on the Palazzo Farnese in Rome, with the former designing the Farnese Palace at Caprarola) methods of moving the famous Heliopolis Obelisk from the Circus Gai et Neronis, where it had been placed by Caligula in 36 C.E., to where it stands today in front of St. Peter's.[17] The task of moving the immense block of stone was finally accomplished some fifty-one years later, under Sixtus V, by the engineer Domenico Fontana — three years after Agrippa presented Gregory XIII with his *Trattato di trasportar la guglia in su la piazza di S. Pietro.*

Though the task — and the glory — of actually moving the obelisk was given to someone else, by any standard, Agrippa's life's work was still prodigious. His work on fencing was only the beginning of a long career: Agrippa was interested in hydraulics (the water-raising system and fountain in the gardens of the Villa Medici in Rome, built by Ferdinando I, son of Cosimo, is his doing),[18] astronomy (the dialogue from the *Trattato di scientia d'arme* was reprinted as *Modo di comporre il moto della sfera* in Rome in 1575 by the heirs of his original printer, Antonio Blado), natural science (*Dialogo sopra la generatione de' venti, baleni, tuoni, fulgori, fiumi, laghi,*

---

17. Agrippa makes this claim in *Trattato di trasportar la guglia,* 5: "Upon my arrival in Rome, which was on October 26, 1535, I wanted to reason out how to transport the obelisk securely and integrally to St. Peter's, and discussed how to do so with that most worthy man Antonio Sangallo and the great MichelAngelo Bonarota [sic]." Both Sangallo (Bramante's student) and Michelangelo were also, in turn, *cappomaestri* of the construction of St. Peter's. See also Filippo Picinelli, *Ateneo dei letterati Milanesi* (Milan, 1670), 100–101.

18. See Leonardo Lombardi, "Camillo Agrippa's Hydraulic Inventions on the Pincian Hill (1574–1578), trans. by Katherine W. Rinne in *The Waters of Rome* 5 (Apr. 2008) http://www.iath.virginia.edu/rome/Journal5LombardiNew.pdf (accessed June 8, 2009).

valli et montagne, published in Rome in 1584 and reprinted in 1598), military science (*Dialogo del modo di mettere in battaglia presto et con facilità il popolo di qual si voglia luogo con ordinanze et battaglie diverse,* dedicated to Henry III of France and published in Rome in 1585), and navigation (*Nuove inventioni sopra il modo di navigare,* Rome, 1595). He also apparently composed an unpublished work on fortifications. Agrippa died in Rome, a very aged man, in about 1595. Antonio Bertolotti, in his *Artisti Lombardi a Roma,* tells us that he was placed with the Congregation of the Virtuosi (*congregazione de' Virtuosi)* in the Pantheon.

HONOR AND ITS DEFENSE IN AGRIPPA'S MILIEU

It is perhaps fitting that Agrippa was once supposed to have been inspired to invent an important fencing technique from watching a cockfight.[19] In his famous article, "Deep Play: Notes on the Balinese Cockfight," Clifford Geertz likewise uses a cockfight as inspiration: "As much of America surfaces in a ball park, on a golf links, at a race track, or around a poker table, much of Bali surfaces

---

19. The technique, the *cavatione,* or disengagement, will be more fully explained below. "G.A.," in his *Pallas Armata* (London, 1639), I.6 says:

> *Cavere* took its beginning from a Cock fight; for *Camillo Agrippa,* a reverend Master of defense at *Rome* fifty years ago (who was the inventor of the Dagger) seeing two Cocks combat together, and observing, how when one of the Cocks leaped up to strike the other with his claw, the other seeing him come leaping at him went quite under him on the other side, conceived that he might make use of this in his Art, and coming home made trial of it, and found it a very useful and remarkable observation.

This is, of course, nonsense with no basis in Agrippa's writings. The first occurrence of this myth is on p. 47 of Hieronimo Calvacabo's *Traité ou instruction pour tirer des armes* (Rouen, 1597, 1617), but translated from an earlier Italian original):

> According to many, Agrippa was the inventor of the pass underneath the sword, having seen two cocks joust together, one of which raised itself up and jumped upon the other in order to peck him, and the other passing underneath to save himself.

in a cock ring. For it is only apparently cocks that are fighting there. Actually, it is men."[20] Difficult as it is for us to imagine in an age when a horror of violence has made the carrying of weaponry so uncouth as to be illegal, to the gentleman of the early modern era, the sword was a fact of life. We might as well imagine modern life without our panoply of personal electronic devices as the sixteenth-century gentleman without his sword. It was an article of dress, a symbol of rank, and a constant companion. At least in theory, the one commodity a gentleman was allowed to trade in — honor — was bought with credit or coin of steel; just as social gaffes and the wrong clothing could make one look the fool, not knowing the etiquette of personal violence could similarly brand one a pariah.

Training in arms was likewise long as essential a component of the education of the gentleman — or man with aspirations to gentility — as riding or dancing. "I judge that the principal and true profession of the courtier ought to be that of arms," states Castiglione's Count Ludovico da Canossa,[21] and princes from Castiglione's patron Guidobaldo da Montafeltro in 1480s Urbino to King Christian IV of Denmark at the turn of the seventeenth century kept household fencing masters (the famous Filipo Vadi and Pietro Monte in the former case; the renowned Salvator Fabris in the latter).[22] This training was hardly limited to the nobility: stolid Parisian burghers kept weapons in their homes and patronized the

---

20. Clifford Geertz, "Deep Play: Notes on the Balinese Cockfight," in *The Interpretation of Cultures* (New York: Basic Books, 1973), 5.

21. *Libro del Cortegiano*, ed. Giulio Carnazzi (Milan: Biblioteca Universale Rizzoli, 1987), 72 (I, 17).

22. On Vadi, see Greg Mele and Luca Porzo's translation of the *Arte gladiatoria dimicandi* (Highland Park, TX: Chivalry Bookshelf, 2002); as for Fabris, Tomasso Leoni has capably translated King Christian's Italian master's 1606 treatise *De lo schermo* as *The Art of Dueling* (Highland Park, TX: Chivalry Bookshelf, 2005). Professor Anglo has discussed Pietro Monte, Vadi's successor at the court of Urbino whom Castiglione also mentions in the *Libro del Cortegiano*, in his "The Man Who Taught Leonardo Darts."

masters of arms whose métier was first recognized by Charles IX in 1569,[23] and at the end of the century, Shakespeare's audience well

---

23. On the keeping of weapons in sixteenth-century France, see Marie-Anne Michaux's excellent MA thesis, "Private Armouries: Arms and Armour in the Parisian Domestic Interior (1515–1547)" (Royal College of Art, 2005). For the guild of Parisian fencing masters, see the third volume of Lespinasse's *Les métiers et corporations de la ville de Paris* (Paris: Imprimere Nationalee, 1897).

It is also to Charles IX that Henri Sainct-Didier, a "Provencal gentleman," and therefore not a member of the guild, dedicated the earliest surviving fencing book to be printed in French, his 1573 *Traicté contenant les secrets du premier livre sur l'espée seule, mère de toutes armes*. Furthermore, it is in Sainct-Didier's treatise that we see the first use in French literature of the term "little flower" for a fencing foil. To quote the dedicatory sonnet that Jean Emery de Berre, "Provencal," writes to the author, whom he also identifies as "Provencal":

Come now all you fencers
Bend your foils [*flourés*] as best you can
Come do honor to the new son of Mars.

Note that Raynouard's *Lexique Roman* (1836) and Levy's *Provenzalisches Supplement-Wörterbuch* do not recognize the orthography *flourés*; rather, they agree that the Provençal for flower is *flor* — not that orthography was anything approaching standard at this point.

The use of the word for "flower" to mean a fencing foil, while a minor one philologically, is of no small importance to the history of fencing, for the *floret*, so named for the buttoned point's resemblance to a flower bud, can be identified with a change to a thrust-oriented method of play in the late sixteenth century. The *Trésor de la Langue Français*, the standard philological authority, gives us the following etymology of this use of *fleuret*:

1580 *floret* (MONTAIGNE, *Essais*, éd. A. Thibaudet, 1. 1 chap. 26, p. 186); 1608 *fleuret* (M. RÉGNIER, *Satyre V* ds *Œuvrs*, éd. G. Raibaud, p. 56). Prob. Adaption de l'ital. *fioretto*, attesté comme terme d'escrime dep. 1598 (Florio d'apr. HOPE, p. 195), proprement "petite fleur" (dep. Dante, *ibid.*), le changement de sens s'expliquany par la resemblance entre le bouton du fleuret et un bouton de fleur (v. *FEW* t. 3, p. 635 a et 637a).

The Florio referred to is the Anglo-Italian scholar John Florio's *A Worlde of Wordes* (1598), in which he gives us as one of the definitions of *fioretti*, "...also foiles to play at rapier and dagger with." De Berre's usage, however, predates

understood Mercutio's mocking references to Italian fencing terms such as *"punto riverso"* and the *"immortal passado"*; that his naming Tybalt "the very butcher of a silk button" was a reference to Rocco Bonetti, an Italian who had moved to London to teach the new style of fencing and who somewhat vaingloriously claimed to be able to hit an Englishman on any button of his doublet; and recognized that Sampson and Gregory were servants by the swords and bucklers they carried in lieu of the aristocratic rapier.[24]

The official recognition of a guild of masters-at-arms actually came rather late in France; the movement had in fact begun in the late fifteenth century as increasingly absolutist rulers, governing territories that came to look increasingly like nation-states and fielding military forces that came to look increasingly like standing armies,

---

Florio, Montaigne, and Hope, but he was not, of course, writing in French (which had taken its modern form at this point), but in Provençal. Despite the fact that De Berre was writing for a Parisian audience who he would have, presumably, wished to understand his writing, we cannot say that the term *floret* was commonly used in French. Sainct-Didier, whose work is the first published French-language fencing treatise, does not make use of it in the rest of the treatise. On the other hand, Cotgrave's *Dictionarie of French and English Tongues* (1611) defines "Floret" as "a foile; or sword with the edge rebated."

The fact that de Berre speaks somewhat derisively of the "foil" that Sainct-Didier mentions nowhere else in his treatise matches well with the sort of fencing Sainct-Didier advocates; much like a Gallic George Silver, he was writing a treatise advocating a conservative, native fashion of fencing in response to the Italian masters, specifically Saviolo, who taught the thrust-oriented mode of fencing that had begun with Agrippa. We can perhaps see his purpose in writing as a defense of the privileges of the Parisian *métier* of the *maîtres in faict des armes* against the influx of foreign teachers. This was, of course, ultimately futile, for the rapier took France by storm.

In speaking of philology, it is also interesting to note that the term *martial art* first appears in the dedicatory poem to the English rapier treatise by G.A., *Pallas armata* (1639).

24. See, for instance, Joan Ozark Holmer's "'Draw if ye be Men': Saviolo's Significance for *Romeo and Juliet,*" *Shakespeare Quarterly* 45.2 (Summer 1994): 163–89 for a full explanation of Shakespeare's use of fencing terminology for both drama and satire.

began to recognize and regulate this quintessentially urban activity. No longer were such guilds (if they may be so-called) of fencing masters merely local organizations, formed by men who, if they had made such teaching their sole profession, were liable to be lumped in with actors, vagabonds, and other such ne'er-do-wells. Rather, they were now granted a certain *dignitas*. In 1478, for instance, Frederick III used his imperial jurisdiction over the cities of the Holy Roman Empire to grant the Frankfurt-based Brotherhood of St. Mark, or *Marxbrüder*, a monopoly on teaching. A similar process had taken place in Spain and the Low Countries by this time, and likewise, Henry VIII granted a royal monopoly on teaching arms to the London Company of Masters of Defense in 1540. It was only in politically disunified Italy that, to the best of my knowledge, no such organizations have been noted. Though the Italians were known for exporting masters-of-arms to the courts of Europe, and though evidence from scattered legal documents and treatises such as Marozzo's provides some tantalizing hints, this is a subject that will require further research.[25]

---

25. See, for instance, "Scuole di scherma in Milano nel 1474" in *Bollettino storico della Svizzera italiana* 7 (1885): 118, in which Johannes Angellus, captain of Milan, arrested a Spanish fencing master for publicly challenging several Milanese masters, one of whom, a Magistro Zentille, is described as the son of ther deceased (quondam) Magistro Pagano. Thanks to Matt Galas for the source.

We gain another image of the teaching of arms in Italy from the following anecdote drawn from Vincent Saviolo's *His Practice* (London, 1595):

And amongst others I will tell you of an accident which hath happened in Padoua, where I my selfe was borne, of a master of Fence called M. Angelo of Alezza, who many yeres brought up, maintained, and taught a nephew of his, in such sort, that hee became a verie sufficient and skilfull man in this art. Which his nephew, whereas by reason should have beene loving and faithfull to him, as to his own father, having so long eaten of his bread, and received from him so many good turnes, especially having bene brought up by him from his childhoode and infancie, he did the quite contrarie, for his uncle Angelo yet living and teaching schollers, hee openly dyd teach and plaie with many, and by that

The popularity of Italian fencing masters in the courts of Europe brings us to another important point. The pedagogy of this art was, as Kate Van Orden makes clear in her recent and excellent *Music, Discipline, and Arms in Early Modern France*,[26] a pervasive and potent symbol of the chain of being. This was seen in the late sixteenth and early seventeenth centuries both at Protestant universities such as Leiden and the Jesuit schools Henri IV patronized for the purposes of educating the *noblesse*. Both the ill-fated Henri III and his successor Henri IV did their parts to try to ensure that fencing would be taught by authorized masters, with the former confirming the guild's regulations in 1585 and the latter encouraging the young noblemen of France to attend the newly-formed and unabashedly royalist Jesuit universities, where fencing and theater were both key components of the curriculum.

---

meanes came acquainted with many Gentlemen, so that hee set up a schoole of Fence, and beganne to teach, entising awaie many which were schollers of his uncle Angelo. A part truly verie vile, and of an unkinde unthankfull man. Whereupon the sayd Angelo complained of this injury and wrong offered by his nephew, to a gentleman who was his scholler and loved him entirely, shewing howe his nephew had not onely impaired his credite, but defrauded him of the aide and helpe which he looked for at his hands, having brought him up, as I have said, and especially being now growen old. Which nephew (as he said) in respect of kindred, bringing up, and teaching of his arte and skill, was bound to have shewed him all friendship and curtesie. Heereupon the Gentleman, Angelo his scholler, promised to seeke redresse, although hee was a friende also unto the nephewe of Angelo. And so, by badde happe, finding the sayde nephew of Angelo, tolde him that for the wrong offered to his master and uncle, he would fight with him, and therewithall put hande to his weapon: the other refused to fight with him because hee was his friend: but the Gentleman tolde him that if hee woulde not defend himselfe hee woulde runne him thorough: as hee dyd in deede, for whilest hee stoode uppon tearmes, and would not do his best to defend himselfe, he ranne him quite thorough the bodie.

26. Chicago: University of Chicago Press, 2005.

The Bourbons and their Spanish Hapsburg counterparts indeed made great use of the didactic power of instruction in the gentlemanly arts. In 1628, Girard Thibault dedicated his *Academie de L'espée* to his patron, Louis XIII.[27] This work, twin to Antoine de Pluvinel's great riding treatise, the *Manège Royale* (both were illustrated by Crispin de Passe), and known as the most sumptuous fencing book ever created, served the dual function of both epitomizing baroque style and valorizing Thibault's system of rapier fence. This art was in turn ultimately derived from a system devised by the Spanish nobleman Jerónimo Sanchez de Carranza in the mid- to late sixteenth century,[28] but in Thibault's case elaborated with illustrations and figures influenced by notions of sacred geometry that implicitly endorsed notions of divine order and the chain of being. Carranza, in turn, was ultimately indebted to Agrippa, as his student, successor, and critic Luis Pacheco de Narváez made clear in a published letter to the duke of Cea dated May 4, 1618:

> Camilo Agripa [sic] was the first to think to reduce [swordsmanship] to a science, to give mathematical demonstrations, and to discuss lines and angles. We need not discuss his scant precision and less than mediocre success, although we will shortly publish on him and other authors. As many of Carranza's concepts originated from that defective text, they were born sickly, little founded in the truth, conflicting with each other, and mostly opposed to common sense and mathematical and natural philosophy.[29]

---

27. Thibault has been translated by John Michael Greer as *Academy of the Sword* (Highland Park, TX: Chivalry Bookshelf, 2007).

28. Carranza's *De la filosophia de las armas* was, according to his own account, written in 1569, but not published until 1582 (in Seville).

29. Luis Pacheco de Narváez, *Carta al duque de cea* (Madrid, 1618), 1–2, translation by Mary Dill Curtis found on the page "Italian Connection" in the *Destreza Translation and Research Project*, http://www.plumes.org/destreza/theory/translations/narvaez_italian.html (accessed Mar. 18, 2008). My thanks to her for the translation (which I have edited for clarity) and original text.

Narváez' attempts to discredit his predecessors, while they made him enemies amongst Carranza's partisans, were not entirely in vain. In 1624, Philip IV named him Head Master of Arms, the chief examiner of the masters who taught the system of fencing in which all Spanish noblemen were trained. (Prior to this, he had been Philip's own fencing master.)[30] In 1643, Louis XIII similarly confirmed the long-standing laws of the Parisian métier, and the following year endorsed detailed instructions for the apprenticeship and testing of new masters-of-arms in seventeen articles.

As great a patron of the art of arms as his father had been, however, it was Louis XIV who gave a royal imprimatur to the métier and raised it to a position of honor by granting it arms and by elevating six of its number to the nobility. As in Spain, the manner of fencing in Paris would thereafter follow the dictates of its licensing board of masters — and there can be no doubt that Louis' preference for the short and elegant court sword that so often appears at his side in portraiture was as much a part of his system of aesthetic control as his dancing the part of the Sun in court ballets.[31]

According to A.V.B. Norman, the custom of wearing the sword with ordinary civilian costume likely began in Spain in

---

30. On this, see Cristóbal Pérez Pastor, *Bibliografía madrileña ó descripción de las obras impresas en Madrid*, 3 (1621–25), reprinted in *Revista de archivos, bibliotecas y museos* (Madrid, 1907): 251. My thanks to Mary Dill Curtis for the reference.

31. The fashion of Versailles remained the European standard for the duration of the *ancien regime* and even after, for, even though the Revolution had made the wearing of swords with male costume as anachronistic as craft guilds, the *syndicat* of masters of arms managed to regain its prestige. Even today the Paris-based Fédération Internationale d'Escrime remains the governing body of the sport into which the Art has decayed. In fact, the exportation of the Revolution meant the end of the ancient fencing guilds east of the frontiers, as well as the Spanish school of fencing on the Penninsula. See below for how fencing could be deployed in the Enlightenment critique of the *métiers*.

the late medieval period.[32] The Spanish term *espada ropera* — the "dress," or more accurately "wearing," sword — is first encountered in the 1468 post-mortem inventory of the goods of Duke Alvaro de Zúñiga. It is this that gave rise to the French term *épée rapière*, which first appears in 1474.[33] Wearing the sword with everyday dress was apparently well-established in Italy as early as 1478: the conspirator Francesco de' Pazzi made sure to embrace Giuliano de' Medici to determine if he wore armor underneath his clothes, but no one remarked upon the sword that Lorenzo wore into the cathedral and with which he would later defend himself as being at all unusual. The Italians simply called this weapon the *spada* or *spada da filo* ("sword with an edge" or "cutting sword"), a term used by Antonio Manciolino possibly as early as 1509, and it is this, a light, straight, double-edged, one-handed, cutting-and-thrusting weapon with a complex hilt, that is essentially Agrippa's weapon.[34]

---

32. That such a custom should originate in Spain, where frontier conditions often prevailed through the era of the *reconquista* and men were granted freeholds in return for military service, should be no surprise. (On this, see Robert Ignatius Burns' various works.) *Hidalgoismo* — and its symbol, the sword — long persisted in Iberian society. As Barthélemy Joly remarked upon the inhabitants of Valladolid in 1603–4: "small craftsmen…unable to do anything else but work for a living…sit disdainfully outside their shops and, for two or three hours in the afternoon, they parade up and down wearing swords." See Barthélemy Joly, *Voyage en Espagne*, in *Revue Hispanique* 20 (1909): 460–618. Translation is Newton Branch's, found in Marcelin Deforneaux, *Daily Life in Spain in the Golden Age*, translated by Newton Branch (Stanford: Stanford University Press, 1979), 43.

33. A.V.B. Norman, *The Rapier and Small-Sword 1460–1820* (New York: Arno Press, 1980), 20.

34. Note that this *spada* (which we are here translating as "rapier" because of the term's wide recognition and Agrippa's thrust-oriented play — function, in other words, taking precedence over form) was not the excessively long weapon that soon came into vogue, but rather a handy one that could be rapidly drawn and deployed. (The term currently in vogue amongst fencing historians, *spada da lato* or "sidesword," is a neologism.) But later weapons were not as long as some think: "King Phillip II issued a law in 1564 that ordered that the sword's length was to be determined by placing the pommel

While the weapon Agrippa employs is not too much of a change from earlier custom, his method of employing it was part of a widening break with the past. Earlier masters, insofar as can be determined from surviving treatises, taught a general-purpose martial art that could applied equally well to the battlefield, the tournament, the vendetta, or the judicial duel. For instance, the master Fiore dei Liberi of Premariacco (fl. c. 1370–1410), in the three known Italian and one Latin manuscripts of his *Fior di Battaglia* (c. 1410),[35] shows not only self-defense against an impromptu dagger attack, but fencing with the longsword,[36] the use of the lance on horseback, defense against a horseman when on foot, and fighting in armor either with poleaxes and other specialized weapons or without. Filipo Vadi, writing in the 1480s, likewise addressed

---

of the weapon in line with the left shoulder and extending the blade across the chest to the end of the middle finger of the laterally extended right arm...the total length of the sword would be approximately 41.25 inches." See Ramon Martinez, "Jeronimo de Carranza's 'Philosophy' of Arms," Martinez Academy of Arms Web site, http://www.martinez-destreza.com/articles/carranza.htm (accessed Mar. 18, 2007).

Likewise, on pp. 278–82 of *Tudor Royal Proclamations*, ed. by Paul L. Hughes and James F. Larkin (New Haven: Yale University Press, 1969), we find regulations concerning fencing schools and blade lengths, tellingly included with those regulating hose-makers (for what was a sword if not a means to distinguish gentlemen from *sans-culottes*?): "Item, her majesty also ordereth and commandeth that no person shall wear any sword, rapier, or suchlike weapon that shall pass the length of one yard and half-a-quarter of the blade at the uttermost, nor any dagger above the length of 12 inches in blade at the most, nor any buckler with any point or pike above two inches in length."

35. Morgan Library M.0383; Getty Museum MS Ludwig XV 13; BnF Lat. 11269 ("Florius de Arte Lutandi"); and the Pisani-Dossi version, now in private hands, which was published by Novati in 1902.

36. The cruciform knightly cutting-and-thrusting weapon, which could be used in one or two hands, and which was in favor from the thirteenth century through the late fifteenth. See Ewart Oakeshott, *The Sword in the Age of Chivalry* (London: Lutterworth Press, 1964; reprint ed., Mineola, NY: Dover Publications, 1996).

unarmored dagger and longsword, as well has how to employ several weapons when armored. Marozzo is less concerned with the classic accoutrements of knighthood — he does not instruct his student on fighting in armor — but he does include battlefield weapons and self-defense against the dagger and an attacker on horseback, and his *spada da filo* is equally well-suited to being carried as either a civilian or military sidearm-cum-mark of rank or being deployed in a judicial combat, which was clearly a major concern for him, as he also authored a lengthy treatise on how such combats ought to be conducted.

Agrippa, on the other hand, is writing for a specific context. His thrusting play is not well-suited to the chaos of the melee, as the Elizabethan polemicist George Silver would later criticize in his 1599 screed *Paradoxes of Defense*. In this work Silver defended the traditional, manly, "English" style of sword-and-buckler fencing — not to mention the prerogatives of the Masters of Defense — against the foppish and fashionable Italian import. Yet Agrippa would likely have agreed with Silver's opinion that "especially in service of the prince, when men shall join together, what service can a soldier do with a rapier, a childish toy wherewith a man can do nothing but thrust, nor that neither, by reason of the length...."[37] Rather, his new form of fencing, Agrippa tells us in his introduction, is for use on the dueling-ground (literally *ne gli steccati*, "within the barriers" or on a closed field) or, somewhat disingenuously, in an "unforeseen armed assault."[38] Agrippa, then, is addressing the use of an entirely *civilian* weapon. The *espada ropera* had become the rapier, a weapon that, as we shall see, is to be used in a new style — one

---

37. George Silver, *Paradoxes of Defence* (London, 1599), 32. http://www. umass.edu/renaissance/lord/pdfs/Silver_1599.pdf (accessed Mar. 13, 2007).
38. Fiore also speaks of his students fighting *in sbara* ("in the barriers") *a oltranza* — though in this period it could refer to either a judicial duel or a tournament with sharp weapons (*combat à outrance* — literally "extreme fighting" — in French chivalric parlance). In practice, of course, these were quite different in that a tournament encounter would be stopped before serious injury occurred, but in terms of nomenclature, they tended to shade together.

befitting a gentleman of a new age. The importance of this new style of weapons use — and the retreat from battle as the trying-ground of valor to the redoubt of the dueling field — cannot be underestimated. Agrippa's subject — and the reception that his style of weapon use received in the courts of Europe — represents a fundamental shift in the nature of elite masculinity that rapidly expanded from the centers of culture to the most rural areas.[39]

The self-conception of the gentry had long been tied up with the conception of man-as-combatant, whether in the tournament lists, in war, or in the vendetta. In a world where the fighting class was the ruling class, there was always something of the aspirational in performing the role of the professional warrior — a fact to which ruling powers were not insensitive. Froissart recounts the incident of 1382 when the burghers of Paris put pressure on the young Charles VI by appearing at the latter's entry into the city armed from head to toe like *droite gens d'armes*.[40] The response was swift and final: "The king overawed the Parisians and the other burghers of northern France, brutally punishing various leaders and demonstrating forcefully that the burghers would not be able to assume the position accorded to 'true men at arms,' even if they had, for a moment, been able to dress the part."[41] The appropriation of the role of the warrior was therefore part of political rhetoric: "The dissatisfied of the world, the ambitious, the disillusioned, and the social radicals all pressed their claims to greater wealth, respect, or authority on their successful use of arms."[42]

Likewise, the famous Paston family may have descended from Norfolk peasantry and lawyers, but as soon as they rose to landed estate, they saw battle as their business — not surprising,

---

39. The often-repeated myth that the rapier was "invented" to penetrate the joints of armor is, of course, ridiculous; the weapon devised for this function, the *estoc*, is morphologically quite different.

40. Jean Froissart, *Oeuvres,* ed by Kervyn de Lettenhove, 25 vols. (Brussels, 1867–77), 10:146–47.

41. Steven Muhlberger, *Deeds of Arms* (Highland, TX: Chivalry Bookshelf, 2005), 14.

42. Muhlberger, 15.

considering that they lived during the Wars of the Roses and that they had to defend their family's newfound wealth both in the courts and by force of arms. The Paston letters are thus filled with references to arms, armor, and fighting. This was no nobility of the robe, but rather hard-headed businesspeople who took for granted that occasionally being involved in violence was part of upper-class status.

South of the Alps, the membrane between town and country-side was more permeable and actual wars were usually fought by (often nobly-born) professionals such as John Hawkwood, Federico da Montefeltro, and Giovanni dalle Bande Nere (father of Cosimo I). However, despite the professional nature of war, citizens of the various Italian communes nonetheless liked to imagine themselves as potential military heroes, as is shown by the taste for art such as Paolo Uccello's *The Battle of San Romano* or Michelangelo's *Battle of Cascina*, or even his famous statue of David, the small but virile warrior, favored by God, who looks over the Alps to defy the transmontane Goliath. Even if Cosimo I, less warlike than his father, did not personally lead his forces, he was fond of martial self-presentation, as can be seen in numerous portraits (notably the one by Bronzino) and the bust of him in antique armor by Cellini — dispelling the spectre of the memory that his illustrious ancestors rose from obscure, bourgeois origins.

Martial self-presentation, then, was no mere fancy, but something deeply imbedded in the culture. *Nobiliare*, to perform nobility, was to *armizare*, to publicly handle weapons, be it in the tournament, in the duel, or in war. As Marco Cavina has remarked, Italian knighthood was defined by a combination of family tradition of equestrian military service with a "knightly" lifestyle, the customs of which were spread by the various courts.[43] This attitude persisted, as Marie-Anne Michaux has noted for France, well into the sixteenth century: "If legally nobility was hereditary, in people's minds it was essentially a function. This 'profession

---

43. Marco Cavina, *Il duello giudiziario per punto d'onore* (Turin: G. Giappichelli, 2003), 9.

of virtue' rested…on chivalric codes elaborated in the previous centuries. As such, anyone performing authentic acts of 'virtue,' in other words showing bravery in battle and skill at arms, could pretend to nobility."[44]

By the time Agrippa wrote, however, this ideology had nonetheless undergone significant and necessary revision from its medieval precedents. As he notes in his dedication to the duke of Florence, "because of the diabolical modern invention of artillery, all that remains to us of the good ancient ways of military honor is the duel." The ongoing military revolution — which may be briefly described as the increased tactical use of gunpowder weapons and well-disciplined massed infantry bodies, the recruitment and maintenance of what were by medieval standards enormous standing armies, and the need for expensive fortifications to counter these measures — not only led to the decline of the small Italian states and the rise of the sort of centralized, absolutist governments that could afford such innovations,[45] but also ended the fantasy of the citizen-soldier.[46] Machiavelli's institution of a Florentine citizen-militia in 1506 was the death rattle of a dying ideal; the militia's rout by Spanish professionals at Prato in 1512 was the last nail in the coffin. This is a world where the most valorous, well-born, and expensively armed knight could meet his death at the hands of an anonymous sniper, as Charles III, duke of Bourbon, did at Rome in 1527.

Many writers have commented on the post-fifteenth-century "decadence" of the Italian military aristocracy, to the point that a lack of martial character became something of a point of national pride.[47] Nonetheless, the idea remained that a military vocation

---

44. See Michaux, 2005.

45. The reduction of the Farnese and Gonzaga states to clients of the Hapsburgs and Valois is a testament to this.

46. For a much fuller and more nuanced discussion of the Military Revolution, see Clifford J. Rogers, ed., *The Military Revolution Debate: Readings on the Military Transformation of Early Modern Europe* (Boulder, CO: Westview Press, 1995).

47. For an excellent historiographical discussion, see Gregory Hanlon's

was the only proper profession for the young aristocrat. "Quite apart from high-minded appeals to princely service or defence of religion, tradition and public opinion sanctioned military careers as the most appropriate natural calling for aristocrats, because it gave them a theater in which to display their bravura and natural generosity, whatever the pretext of the war," as Gregory Hanlon has noted.[48] But the field of honor was not to be found by plowing one's own acre. With Italian city-states reduced to second-class powers, unable to raise forces comparable to the massive French and Hapsburg armies, martially-inclined nobility were instead inclined to take service in the armies of foreign princes. The domestic path to upward mobility was the courts of the powerful.

This brings us to the private duel of honor between individuals, which was a uniquely *Italian* and *courtly* phenomenon. Spain may have birthed the rapier, but it suffered a dearth of native "doctors of honor" (del Castillo being the notable exception).[49] The famous Italian *condotierre* Francesco Maria della Rovere, duke of Urbino, claimed to have invented the specific form of the challenge,[50] and, significantly, the small courts of Emilia-Romagna and Lombardy were, according to Cavina, "particularly fertile for men-at-arms, professors-of-arms, and for dueling fields [*campi franchi*]."[51] The duel was a martial role that was at once intimately personal and completely respectable to play on the stage of public opinion, as can be seen by Charles V's famous challenge to François I.

Agrippa's ideas concerning personal combat quite clearly bespeak this channeling of martial inclinations away from factional conflict and the Augustinian "just war" undertaken at behest of

---

"The Decline of a Provincial Military Aristocracy: Siena 1560–1740," *Past and Present* 155 (May 1997): 64–108.
48. Hanlon, 154–55.
49. Cavina, 191.
50. Cavina, 127 and Appendix 3.
51. Cavina, 125. For a study of the rather expensive fortifications of Mantua, see Thomas F. Arnold, "Fortifications and the Military Revolution: The Gonzaga Experience" in Rogers, 201.

the prince, into the duel.[52] This was class intimately tied up with ambition: carrying weapons, practicing the use of weapons, and occasionally employing them in earnest, is, again, a performance of rank. If it were a performance, though, the theater was one owned by the ruling authority. The increasing number of prescriptive, authoritative texts on honor and dueling — notably Girolamo Muzio's 1550 *Il Duello* — were the script.[53] Muzio, a noted Roman *literato*, was, like Agrippa and Annibale, apparently equally concerned with both sword and pen, and like many contemporary writers had likewise sought Cosimo's patronage, sending him a copy of *Il Duello* in 1551.[54] For a book to be dedicated to this great prince was, of course, nothing unusual, and part of Cosimo's

---

52.   Interestingly, many authorities, such as Pigna in his 1554 treatise *Il Duello*, hold the duel as a more dangerous and therefore honorable test than battle, as well as one that puts a premium on skill over luck. See Frederick R. Bryson's classic study, *The Sixteenth-Century Italian Duel* (Chicago: University of Chicago Press, 1938); and Tommaso Leoni, "Notes on the Judicial Duel in Italy" (paper presented at the International Swordfighting and Martial Arts Convention, Lansing, MI, Aug. 3–6, 2006, published at http://www.salvatorfabris.com/forum/viewtopic.php?t=104url (accessed Mar. 18, 2007)).

Another forum for masculine performance and martial self-perception, and one closely related to the duel, was the tournament. *Contra* Maurice Keen's idea of the "Indian summer" of sixteenth-century chivalry, "as if the vein of fresh ore had become at last exhausted, so that the moneyers could do no more than remint old coin" (*Chivalry* (New Haven: Yale University Press, 1984), 268), the tournament remained vital and important in Italy through the early modern period.

53.   The preeminent authority on the rise, development, and decline of this form of combat is Marco Cavina's *Il duello giudizario per punto d'onore*. Another valuable work (albeit on seventeenth-century Bologna) is Giancarlo Angelozzi's *La nobiltà disciplinata* (Bologna: CLUEB, 2003); nor should Claudio Donati *L'idea di nobiltà in Italia* (Rome: Laterza, 1988) be omitted.

54.   Muzio's letter is preserved in the Archivio di Stato di Firenze, Mediceo del Principato 401, f. 151. On Muzio and the Gonzagas, see Julia L. Hairston, "Out of the Archive: Four Newly-Identified Figures in Tullia d'Aragona's *Rime della Signora Tullia di Aragona et di diversi a lei* (1547)," *MLN* 118.1 (Jan. 2003): 257–63.

business as a ruler was, of course, overseeing duels of honor. However, it should also be noted that the Gonzagas were Muzio's patrons just as the Farnese were Annibale Caro's — Muzio was a secretary of Ferrante Gonzaga's. This raises the fascinating possibility of Agrippa's *Trattato* being a "Farnese" response to the "Gonzaga" *Il Duello*, with both appealing to Cosimo as a sort of arbiter, since, as in a duel, he was a sort of neutral third authority (as will be discussed below). Equally likely was that dedicating the work to a cardinal would have been impolitic, as the Council of Trent, which Alessandro Farnese supported, would shortly condemn dueling.[55]

The other traditional outlet for violent energies in Italy besides the duel was, of course, the vendetta, such as the generations-long conflict between the Savorgnan, Zambarlani, and Strumieri factions in the backwaters of sixteenth-century Friuli.[56] As Daniel Lord Smail has remarked, the feud, the vendetta, the duel, and the lawsuit, though they might take different forms, proceed from similar impulses.[57] However, the vendetta bespeaks a weak central authority and the comparative power of factions consolidated around patronage networks.[58] Accordingly, the vendetta was on its way out as state power consolidated in this period. On the other hand, the duel of the early to mid-sixteenth century, as practiced in Italy, tended to enhance a ruler's prestige.

To judge from the stringent stipulations, duels should have occurred with much less frequency than they did: there had to

---

55. Altoni's unpublished work, written in perhaps 1536, was also dedicated to Cosimo, whom he identifies as his "patron." Presumably, Altoni was his household fencing master. However, Altoni was quite possibly deceased by the time Agrippa wrote.

56. Edward Muir, *Mad Blood Stirring* (Baltimore: Johns Hopkins University Press, 1993).

57. Daniel Lord Smail, "Factions and Vengeance in Renaissance Italy: A Review Article," *Comparative Studies in Society and History*, 38.4 (Oct. 1996): 781–89.

58. One should not confuse faction with kin group. Consider the famous case of Guglielmo de' Pazzi running madly about the Duomo, protesting he had no knowledge of the conspiracy.

be an accusation on the part of the plaintiff that the defendant — who had to be of equal or lesser rank and physically capable of fighting — had done something contrary to honor. The initial injury could not be provable through witnesses or tried through a court — thus generating a "hidden truth" that must be brought to light. The next step would be for the defendant to "give the lie" to the plaintiff's accusation, whereupon the plaintiff would issue a *cartello*, a precisely written, notarized, and public letter signed by witnesses and vetted by the judicial authorities that would set out the defendant's real or imagined crimes and invite him to meet in battle. This would be followed by a reply from the defendant, who could recuse for good cause — but this would hardly be putting forth a *bella figura!*

Choice of weapons fell to the defendant. These could be any arms in common use, civilian or military, that both had the capacity to wield — including horses and armor. However, public opinion considered the use of offensive weapons alone, without the benefit of armor — such as was the case with Agrippa's rapier fence — to be most honorable, as it maximized the opportunity to display one's own *virtù* (manliness) and downplayed the ameliorating effects of luck and wealth. This transformation had been going on for some time. Already in 1509, Pietro Monte was railing against the duel in shirtsleeves *(en camisa)* on the grounds that it did not conform to military usage.[59] Agreeing with the legal tradition established by jurists such as Giovanni di Legnano and Baldo di Ubaldi and both vulgarized and elaborated upon by Paris de Puteo in 1470s Naples,[60] Monte wrote that one ought to do battle on a field granted by the prince, protected by the sorts of armor that were customarily used in a military context, not stripped bare and armed with only a sword. Nonetheless, the preference for this form of combat is seen clearly in the increasing production and consumption of treatises on swordsmanship such as Marozzo's and Agrippa's that emphasized combat in shirtsleeves.

---

59. Anglo, "The Man who Taught Leonardo Darts," 266.
60. Cavina, 90–91.

Within forty days of the initial challenge, the two principals would meet a few hours before sunset at the *campo franco*, a field set up on land granted by a lord neutral to both parties (the securing of which was the responsibility of the plaintiff), or else *alla macchia*, on public lands, and enter into the *steccato*, the palisaded area where the duel would take place. Only the judge, the combatants, and their two seconds *(padrones)* were allowed into the *steccato*; spectators, who usually included the lord who had granted the field and his retinue, were warned to remain quiet under pain of death by the herald whose job it was to read the formal charges. The temporal boundaries were from the time the herald blew his trumpet to one of several predetermined occurrences: the sun's setting, one of the combatants touching the *steccato* with his back, one or both suffering incapacitating wounds, or one or both dying. The duel thus occurred in an artificial time and place, walling off the parties' conflict from the rest of society. It also took place under artificial rules: the accuser had the right of the first blow, and such subterfuges as striking the enemy's horse, grappling, and producing hidden weapons were highly disapproved of or even illegal. Honor, again, was in the performance.[61]

Such was the practice of the legally recognized Italian "judicial duel for point of honor" (as Cavina terms it) before the decrees of the Council of Trent drove the practice underground in the last four decades of the sixteenth century. While ostensibly held to determine truth, the duel was also thought to make hidden *virtú* manifest — as will be amply discussed below, where we examine the aesthetics of Agrippa's martial art. If we see it in the light of game theory, it was a positive-sum game where both parties staked their lives for a gain of honor (possibly mutual, if both performed well). In such a case then it certainly falls under the rubric of Huizinga's "serious play."[62] Whereas medieval man could be litigious in matters of honor, early modern man was — at least in his own self-image

---

61. All per Leoni (2006); and Muir, 167. Leoni uses Pigna as his main source.

62. Johan Huizinga, *Homo Ludens* (Boston: Beacon Press, 1971).

— pugnacious.[63] However, this form of sanctioned violence also tended to work towards the authority of the state, both because it tended to sublimate destructive conflict between groups into limited conflicts between individuals and because courts and rulers were seen as having the authority to approve *cartelli* and grant arenas for battle.

But if it tended to work towards state power, this particular ritual was not an imposition from the top down, but rather a collusion between the various layers of society. Duelists formed a market for *campi franchi* and rulers controlled the supply. The new ethos of the private quarrel gave a publicly acknowledged and much-desired outlet for martial self-expression — and thus social capital — to men who would not have formerly been considered part of the warrior-aristocracy. The market for dueling was expanded by the fact that Agrippa's unarmored rapier fence was radically democratic. While suitable for aristocrats by virtue of both its scientifically rationed theorems and the greater danger it presented to the combatants (and thus the greater degree of bravery that it required), the rapier duel did not require strapping on expensive armor or mounting a similarly pricey trained warhorse. It did not matter how skilled one was at riding — the traditional knightly skill upon which victory in equestrian combat was dependent, and which required years of training, rather than the given maximum of forty days. In the last chapter of the *Trattato* (II, 26), ostensibly treating with combat on horseback, Agrippa merely states "I can not give certain rules for any science, not having sufficiently studied the art since, due to the ever-increasing inconvenience, I have not been able to practice fighting on horseback" — hardly the attitude of a *cavallero!* [64] One's sword, wit, and *virtú* were all that was required

---

63. For the former tendency, see especially Daniel Lord Smail, *The Consumption of Justice: Emotions, Publicity, and Legal Culture in Marseille, 1264–1423* (Ithaca: Cornell University Press, 2003).

64. Despite Agrippa's unwillingness to rationalize fencing on horseback, it should be noted that his contemporary Frederico Grisone was attempting to reduce the training of horses to a system.

— an attitude well suited to such a self-made, upwardly-mobile, and frankly, egotistical man as Agrippa.

AGRIPPA'S AUDIENCE

Like authors of every age, Agrippa assumes that his reader will have a certain relationship to the text — a fact that, in turn, informs his work. Tied into this is the question of why we possess relatively few books in this genre: even considering accidents of survival, given the ubiquity of training in arms, one would think that works on fencing would be relatively common. Yet only some two score manuscripts and four (Spanish) printed works from before 1500 are known. The number of printed titles (including reprints) from the sixteenth century amount to roughly half this number, together with a number of manuscripts (though, of course, more examples of any particular printed work are existent).[65] We have no printed works in English before 1595, and that by Saviolo, an Italian.

If we examine the matter more closely, however, the reason for the relative rarity of fencing books becomes more apparent. The writing of a treatise on fencing requires several presuppositions, namely a class of literate consumers who have a desire to learn to manage weapons; relative independence from a guild system, or at least a guild system that does not discourage leaving records of its teachings (which in turn depends on local political conditions); a monetized economy (which is to say an urbanized economy) that will support professional teachers of arms; and, most importantly, the teacher himself must be both motivated and sufficiently educated to craft a book. (It is also worth noting that then, as now, most masters only wrote after a lifetime's experience.)

---

65.   It is difficult to quantify the number with any certainty, as some cannot be precisely dated and new manuscripts are always being discovered. Note that this is not inconsistent with the survival of arms and armor: more utilitarian items are less likely to be preserved for posterity. My thanks to Steve Hick for helping me to make a census.

Given that a certain base level of education is needed to write a book on fencing, it should be no surprise that the particular rhetoric of any particular work should follow the pedagogical model of its time. While professional teachers of swordsmanship can be documented as far back as the twelfth century, invariably in an urban milieu (indeed, our evidence for their existence comes from municipal governments' attempts to ban the profession as an activity liable to give rise to social disruption), the earliest surviving technical work on fencing, a manuscript written in southern Germany c. 1325[66] depicts a priest and a woman named Walpurgis giving lessons in sword-and-buckler play to students wearing clerical habits, and was likely written in the milieu of a cathedral school.[67] Besides this manuscript, a rich German medieval tradition of *Fechtbucher* ("fencing" or "fighting" books) survives. Many of these were scribed by the disciples of the fourteenth-century master Johannes Liechtenauer, who passed on his teachings in cryptic *merkversen* (mnemonic sayings). The Liechtenauer tradition was evidently a literary as well as a martial one; for instance, Hanko Döbringer, the student who first wrote down Liechtenauer's teachings[68] in 1389, was a priest. Other German teachers were also lettered. One, Johannes Lecküchner (c. 1430s–1482) was, like Döbringer, a priest, and some were apparently Jews. A 1459 manuscript of Hans Talhoffer's *Fechtbuch* depicts a Jew teaching Hebrew letters,[69]

---

66. B.L. Cotton MS I.33
67. I.33 today resides at the Royal Armouries in Leeds, and has been reproduced in facsimile and translated by Jeffrey L. Forgeng as *The Medieval Swordsman's Art: A Facsimile and Translation of Royal Armouries MS I.33* (Union City, CA: Chivalry Bookshelf, 2003). Karl E. Lochner, in his *Die Entwicklungsphasen der europäischen Fechtkunst* (Vienna: Selbstverlag des Verfassers, 1953), mentions a manuscript by the Milanese Del Serpente brothers that may date from 1295; no such treatise has ever been uncovered.
68. Germanisches Nationalmuseum Nürnberger Handschrift Cod. HS 3227a.
69. *Hans Talhoffers Alte Armatur und Ringkunst* (MS Thott 290 2, Kongelige Bibliothek, Copenhagen).

and another manuscript from the 1450s by Jud Lew, a Jew named "lion," today resides in the library of the University of Augsburg.[70]

The same goes for Italy: Fiore dei Liberi, who dedicated his work to the d'Este family of Ferrara and claimed to have fought several unarmored matches (or duels) with sharps against jealous rivals, was also obviously an educated man able to buck the usual path to mastery due to his social station and powerful connections. Vadi, of course, worked in the court of Urbino, one of the most noted centers of literary production and the birthplace of the early modern courtly ideal that melded the scholarly with the martial. Pietro Monte, who was also employed at Urbino, produced most of his works in manuscript in the 1480s and '90s, and was apparently a theologian in addition to being a teacher of the arts of combat. Similarly, it is likely no coincidence that Manciolino, Marozzo, and the author of the early sixteenth-century "Anonimo Bolognese" manuscript were Bolognese, given the influence of the university and its students on the city's culture.

The changes the print revolution wrought in fencing texts are obvious. Unlike scholastic treatises, patristic writings, legal codices, or other relatively widely-copied texts, manuscripts such as Fiore's or those in the Liechtenauer tradition were never intended for general distribution, but rather for a limited audience who had already received tuition from the master who composed the work. The fine hand, carefully planned layout, use of gold leaf, and rich use of pigments in Fiore's or Vadi's manuscripts, for instance, are more similar to books of hours commissioned by a single wealthy patron than they are to more quotidian texts. They are therefore most emphatically not didactic "teach yourself" manuals, such as the modern reader would expect, but rather memory-books of

---

70. Universitätsbibliothek Augsburg Cod.I.6.4.3. For a Jew to teach swordsmanship may not have been so unusual; after all, the profession was an unsavory one in this period. There are records, for instance, of Jewish fencing masters in thirteenth-century England. See Paul Brand, "The Jewish Community in the Records of English Royal Government" in *The Jews in Medieval Britain: Historical, Literary and Archaeological Perspectives,* ed. by Patricia Skinner (Rochester, NY: Boydell & Brewer, 2003).

the sort discussed by Mary Carruthers — that is, an aid to preserve knowledge.[71] As Fiore says, "without books, no one can be a good teacher or student of this art.... there's so much to this art that there isn't a man in the world with such a good memory that he can remember a quarter of it."[72] The key phrase here is *remembering* (*tener a mente*, literally "to bear in mind"), not learning — and if we read between the lines, we can see Fiore's assertion as a slap in the face of the more numerous, more traditional masters who did *not* write.

On the other hand, the rhetoric of the printed work is quite different, as its intended audience is exponentially larger than a manuscript's could ever have been. This broader group of consumers could not be presupposed to have familiarity with the author's teachings. Sixteenth-century printed works on fencing, which require the author to articulate his ideas to a reader presumably unknown to him, therefore tend to be much more comprehensive in their explanations than were the previous two centuries' manuscripts. While still requiring a prior knowledge of fencing — one cannot learn such a complicated physical art from a book — they did serve to enhance the author's prestige by showing the superiority of his practice, as well as serving as an aid to the student. However, writers were slow to realize the full possibilities of this new form of media. Manciolino addresses his *giocatore* (literally, "player," but perhaps better rendered as "fencer"), but he seeks no further goal than to set down the rules of a wholly conventional system of fencing, and Marozzo, as stated previously, is even more conservative, speaking directly to the master.[73]

---

71. See Mary J. Carruthers, *The Book of Memory* (Cambridge: Cambridge University Press, 1990).

72. Pierpont-Morgan MS M.383 Folio 2r, l. 40–41; transcript found at http://www.the-exiles.org/FioreProject/Project.htm (accessed Apr. 7, 2007).

73. Again, neither Altoni or the Anonimo Bolognese, while they remain good sources on actual *practice*, made it into print.

Agrippa, on the other hand, truly exploited the possibilities of the print revolution.[74] His *Trattato* is the first of a new sort of fencing book — a *treatise*, a work that sought to increase its authors' fame by widely sharing knowledge, illustrating and systematizing the principles of an art. In doing so, he opens up the possibility of breaking with tradition. After all, he has nothing to lose by being a revolutionary; unlike Marozzo, who is at least ostensibly writing for professional, guild-authorized pedagogues, Agrippa speaks directly to the student, arguing from first principles a new method for doing things. In breaking with the past, Agrippa appealed to a second group of readers less obvious than potential patrons such as Alessandro Farnese or Cosimo I — namely, an entire emerging class of self-made men outside of traditional power structures, such as aristocratic families and guilds, who were nonetheless eager to better themselves by martial performance. In other words, they were the same individuals who formed the market for the "judicial duel for point of honor." This is still a limited audience — as we shall see, his work is replete with references specific to a certain textual community — but the political import cannot be ignored.

Agrippa's ideas on the nature of Authority and the authority of Nature are neatly encapsulated by the frontispiece, which pictures him seated at a table, holding his own in debate with Scholastic philosophers clearly designated by their robes and caps. In Agrippa's right hand is a divider, used for making empirical measurements of natural phenomena; his left rests on an armillary sphere, used for making physical demonstrations of his ideas concerning the structure of the universe. At his side is a sword; beneath his foot is the globe, and below that, on the floor, are sketched a geometrical diagram and another sword, suggesting that the principles underlying both fencing and astronomy — for mastering the human sphere and the cosmic — are the same. On the shelf above Agrippa are a

---

74. Arguably, Francesco di Sandro Altoni attempted the same in his early sixteenth-century *Monomachia,* but his work was, as far as we know, never printed until Alessandro Battistini, Massimo Rubboli, and Iacopo Venni edited it as *Monomachia: Trattato dell'arte di scherma* (Rimini: Il Cerchio, 2007).

divider and an angle for making measurements oneself, while the reigning principle above the philosophers are the dry, dusty (and presumably Latin) books from which they draw their arguments. Ruling all is an hourglass representing time. No more concise statement of the emerging empirical mindset can be imagined, or of the sixteenth-century confidence in human reason. The implications of Agrippa's writing such a work are similar to those of Denis Diderot incorporating the fencing treatise of Domenico Angelo, a non-member of the Parisian *métier* who taught fencing and riding to the elite of England, into his *Encyclopedia* some two centuries later. Not only does it de-privilege traditional (which is to say guild) ways of knowing in favor of the democracy of the printing press, it is an implicit challenge to the existing power structure in favor of a more rational order favorable to the self-made man and derived from observation of Nature.[75]

Revolutionary though Agrippa's intentions may have been, thanks to the fashion for the duel *all'italiana* — as well as the fact that the rapier did the job it was supposed to do frighteningly well — within a generation after his writing the European aristocracy had come to accept Agrippa's rapier as the sidearm of the gentleman, even though the judicial duel in all its punctilios was not practiced outside of Italy. English writers such as Shakespeare in *Romeo and Juliet* and Sir Philip Sidney in his *Astrophil and Stella*, played on the perceived difference between the upper-class, Continental thrusting rapier and George Silver's beloved, common, native English cutting sword in what Kenneth Hodges has called a sort of "chivalric convection."[76] Likewise, despite the kings of France refusing to grant *champs clos* to anyone in the aftermath of the 1547 La Chataigneraie-Jarnac debacle, the stolid bourgeois of

---

75. Diderot was roundly criticized for this by Danet in the latter's 1766 treatise. On the political import of this, see William H. Leckie, Jr.'s forthcoming work on fencing and the Enlightenment.

76. Kenneth Hodges, "Chivalric Convection: Sir Philip Sidney's Response to Popular Fencing." Paper presented at the International Congress on Medieval Studies, Kalamazoo, MI, 2006. See also his forthcoming monograph on *Popular Chivalry and Tudor Nationalism*.

Paris still imitated their betters by keeping rapiers and other such weapons in their homes (though military weapons such as halberds were more common)[77] and some twelve years after, Charles IX still saw fit to establish the métier for those who taught their use.[78] Even the Germans saw fit to adopt the rapier, grafting it onto a venerable academic tradition of fencing.[79] Learning rapier fencing, in other words, became part of "courtesy."

The rhetoric of Agrippa's *Trattato* also rather tends to support Muir's case that the duel grew not out of Christian mores or the judicial repression of feuding, but rather new ideas of how the individual should act in society — the mannerism of the gentleman of the court, rather than the valor of the knight or the vengeance of the wronged paterfamilias. "The rules for the duel created a script for an extended, almost theatrical performance that channeled the dangerous anger of the participants into a series of formalities that disarmed opponents until they could meet on the dueling ground."[80] It is an artifact of a masculinity of courtly manners in an age of increasing absolutism, not a masculinity of factional vendettas and revenge as Muir described for the early sixteenth century.

The cause for this necessary shift in social values can be seen as the decline of the political role of factions based on agnatic kinship and patronage in the face of the increasing power of despots such as Cosimo I and their courts as the path to all wealth and advancement — or, in Agrippa's Rome, the dependence of a client class on the spoils system of the corrupt pre-Reformation Church, as distributed by such dynasties as the Farnese.[81] The rise of the

---

77. Michaux, 2005..

78. Lespinasse, 3:599–600.

79. See, for instance, Joachim Meyer of Strausbourg's *Gründliche Beschreibung* of 1570, translated by Jeffrey Forgeng as *The Art of Combat: A German Martial Arts Treatise of 1570* (New York: Palgrave Macmillan, 2006) where the rapier appears next to a longsword tradition that may be traced to the fourteenth-century master Johannes Liechtenauer.

80. Muir, 167.

81. Yet, lest we forget, factionalism still remained, incorporated into this schema: the feud between Caro and Castelvetro and their dependents began with a poem praising the house of Valois.

despots, in turn, can be traced by the necessary consolidation of states in the wake of the military revolution. Ultimately, the duel for the point of honor grew out of the combined ambitions of self-made courtiers and rulers to promote their own prestige and interests at the expense of those of the old elite. It helped to limit the damage done by factional violence, and, despite its later illegality, ultimately benefited state-building.[82] Such are the ironies of history.

STRUCTURE OF THE WORK

We can now turn to the content of the work itself. Published in Rome in 1553 by the papal printer Antonio Blado, successor to Ludovico Arrighi,[83] the *Trattato di scientia d'arme* is surprisingly small in size — some 6.5 by 7 inches[84] and perhaps a half-inch thick. The chancery italic font, engraved capitals, and fine paper mark it as a high-quality item, even if the printers could have used a good copyeditor (there is, for example, no chapter 8). The *motu propio* signed by "Ph[illip] Salutiarum" (that is, the Papal Vicar-General Fillipo Archinto) preceding Agrippa's work proper serves as a copyright, forbidding any unauthorized reproduction for ten years. The work was a great success, and a new edition was produced in Venice by Pinargenti in 1568 (who also republished Marozzo in that same year) and again, also in Venice in 1604 by Roberto Meglietti.[85]

---

82. François Billacois, in his *Le Duel dans la société française des XVIe–XVIIe siècles. Essai de psychosociologie historique* (Paris: École des Hautes Études en Sciences Sociales, 1986), makes the opposite point for France in the seventeenth century: that it was a form of self-destructive resistance to absolutism.

83. Stanley Morison, *Four Centuries of Fine Printing,* 4th ed. (New York: Barnes & Noble, 1960), p. 26.

84. The copies of the first printing that I have examined at the Pierpont Morgan Library and the Royal Armouries in Leeds, as well as a copy belonging to Malcolm Fare, editor of the British fencing magazine *The Sword,* had been somewhat reduced by rebinding

85. See Giorgio Enrico Levi and Jacopo Gelli, *Bibliografia del duello* (Milan: Ulrico Hoepli, 1903), 102–3.

The Blado edition evidently went through at least two print runs, as two illustrations differ between surviving copies. The diagram in 1.14 is replaced in some copies with a more accurate representation of the technique under discussion, and the original engraving of a young Agrippa is also replaced with a later engraving of an older and more respectable-looking likeness of the author. Mr. Fare theorizes that after the book's initial success, the portrait was re-done by an artist with a finer hand for a second print run. This explanation seems plausible.[86]

According to Ruth Mortimer's *Catalogue of Books and Manuscripts*, the fifty-five copperplate engravings illustrating the work — fifty-three fencing figures and two allegorical scenes —have been variously attributed to Leonardo da Vinci (though the influence of Leonardo's thought is evident, the idea that he inscribed the plates is, of course, ridiculous — Leonardo died in 1519), the school of Marc' Antonio Raimondi (who died in the 1530s), and — more likely — Jan van der Straet, also known as Giovanni Stradano or Stradanus, who was an associate of Salviati.[87] The sixteenth-century art chronicler Giovan Paolo Lomazzo, for his part, claimed Carlo Urbino (to whom Panofsky also attributes the Codex Huygens in the Morgan Library).[88] A seventeenth-

---

86. Private correspondence between myself and Malcolm Fare.

87. Ruth Mortimer, *Catalogue of Books and Manuscripts* (Cambridge, MA: Harvard University Press, 1964), 2:6. Brunet suggests the school of Marc Antonio in his *Manuel du librarie et de l'amateur de livres* (Paris: Librarie de Firmin Didot Freres, 1860–78); Ragghianti hypothesizes van der Straet in his "Scherma con geometrica," *Critica d'arte* 147–49 (1976): 188. Gelli published an article in the Milan magazine *La Lettura* (Dec.1, 1901): 1113–21, denying Michelangelo's hand in the matter.

88. Sergio Marinelli, "The Author of the Codex Huygens," *Journal of the Warburg and Courtauld Institutes* 44 (1981): 214–20 at 218. The Lomazzo reference is found on p. 230 of his *Rime* (Milan, 1587). Giuseppe Cirillo, in his "Postille a Carlo Urbano e osservazioni sulla puttura cremasca dal '500 in relazione con Genova," *Parma per l'arte* 13 (2007): 25–46, also argues that it was Urbino on the basis of a preparatory study for the frontispiece now in the collection of the Istituto e Museo di Storia della Scienza in

Fig. 1. Inscription Attributed to Torquato Tasso on Mr. Fare's Copy.

century inscription on a copy of Agrippa's *Trattato* supposedly in the hand of Torquato Tasso ascribes the engravings to Michelangelo, but this is spurious. This copy, which Brunet mentions in the fifth edition of his *Manuel du libraire et de l'amateur de livres* as having been owned by Joseph Molini, librarian to the duke of Tuscany, is now in the possession of Mr. Fare, who has generously allowed us to reproduce the engravings for this translation.[89] The 1568 Pinargenti edition does not replicate the original artwork. In his introduction, the engraver Giulio Fontana claimed that the plates had so degraded with age as to be unusable, and so he prepared new engravings — which, alas, cannot be judged to be the equals of the originals. Fontana also did not seek to replicate the allegorical scenes, which, as we shall see, are key to a full understanding of Agrippa's work.[90]

In any case, the identity of the artist(s) of 1553 is not terribly important; the genius behind the illustrations was Agrippa's, and the engraver was his instrument. Aesthetically, the engravings belong to the peak of Renaissance design. Their sinuous, twisting

---

Florence — though there is no basis in Agrippa's text for Cirillo's identification of the other seated figure as Annibale Caro.

89. Mortimer, 6. See also the frontispiece.

90. Briost, Drévillon, and Serna, on p. 139 of their otherwise quite good *Croiser le Fer* (Seyssel: Champ Vallon, 2002), maintain that Fontana also executed the original engravings.

forms, lent a sculptural quality by a masterful use of hatching, are no doubt influenced by Michelangelo — remember, this was Rome of the 1550s — but, as we shall see, this is not decadent Mannerist form without function. In their dynamism, balance, and grace, they echo the effect Agrippa and his students must have had in action, just as the harmony and proportions of Baroque portraiture are the counterpart to the stately rhythm of a minuet or the frenzied energy of a Jackson Pollock painting echoes an Orff composition — or, for that matter, Andy Warhol's silkscreen series of consumer products such as Campbell's Soup and Marilyn Monroe mirror the mass-market rebellion of rock music.

Though Agrippa speaks of adversaries taking to the dueling-field — the *stecatto* — all actions in the engravings take place in a sort of null space, an idealized fighting-ground. Likewise, the figures are classically nude; this is Man stripped down to his essentials. The art of fencing is a sort of abstract, neutral knowledge, unburdened by cultural ideas of trial by combat. Through Fortune is not absent, this is a Platonic form of fighting that can be applied in any situation. Later, when Agrippa demonstrates more applied technique, such as how to seize an opponent's weapon or arm, how to apply his principles with sword and round-shield, or with battlefield weapons such as halberds and two-handed swords, the combatants are clothed in antique costumes and contemporary clothes. (Interestingly, in the plate for II, 19, where Agrippa shows how a small man can throw a larger, the larger contestant seems to be dressed as a German landsknecht — not surprising, considering the lasting legacy of the Sack of Rome and the Farnese faction's antipathy to imperial interests.)

The structure of Agrippa's *Trattato* is as well-planned as St. Peter's Basilica. The papal copyright and a dedication to the duke of Florence are followed by a short preface in which Agrippa explains that he does not need a long preface to explain his "new invention":

> ...since from part to part, following the logical order of the work, it will be made obvious in the third part. This

consists of application, and is very different from the writings from which it is derived. For this reason it is necessary that everyone who wishes for honor in whichever Science and Art, having been well apprised of the Theory, makes it come alive with Practice....

In the initial section of this tripartite division, Agrippa explains his reasoning for the division of the work, giving a vocabulary of actions and grammar of rules to follow when fencing; in the second, he combines these simple actions into more complicated forms; in the third, he puts them together into practical application. He thus begins from first principles with an explanation of the *guardie*, that is, offensive-cum-defensive positions. Whereas previous writers had a multiplicity of *guardie* — Marozzo lists twelve — Agrippa reduced this to four positions upon which all other actions are based. Agrippa's system of *guardie*, it should be mentioned, remains the basis for the numbering of hand positions in the Italian method of fencing down to the present day.

Agrippa also discards those postures that remove the point of the sword from the opponent, reasoning that, as the closest distance between two points is a straight line, the thrust is the quickest and most efficacious technique to use in defending oneself. To quote Briost, Drévillon, and Serna, "...he in fact transposed the logic of the economy of means that he already practiced in construction and replaced it by an economy of actions."[91] Furthermore, as the Roman military theorist Vegetius said — and Agrippa would no doubt have been aware — a thrust penetrates the thoracic cavity, whereas a cut may be superficial; moreover, a circular cut exposes the arm and right side to a counterattack. Likewise, a quicker, deceptive thrust may be given before it is seen.[92] This is not a new

---

91. Briost, Drévillon, and Serna, 146.
92. *De Re Militari*, I, 12: ...they are taught not to cut but to thrust with the sword, for the Romans not only easily vanquish, but even mock those who cut with the sword. The reason why is that a cut, no matter how strongly it is given, does not frequently kill, since the vital parts and bones are armored

concept — as Altoni says, "The point is the most important of all the blows because it is the quickest, easiest, and the most secure" and advocates continually directing the point at the adversary[93] — unlike earlier writers, Agrippa does not have us begin with the sword drawn back to make a very strong attack, but rather has us push the thrust forwards with the lower body. Furthermore, since this is not a system that one would use in armor, there is no need to increase the power of the blow by starting with the sword cocked over one's shoulder.

Rather than referring to ancient authorities, however, Agrippa instead gives us a geometrical proof of the efficacy of the thrust.[94] Considering the body as a machine constructed along the proportions given by Vitruvius — whose influence on the work is discussed below — and using this analysis to break down the component movements of the thrust, Agrippa explains that as one extends one's arm and increases the length of one's stride, one can increase the range of one's attack. While seemingly simplistic, this is the first full explanation in a published work of what eventually became known as the fencing lunge.[95] That the diagram should also resemble a Cartesian coordinate system should be no surprise, for Descartes, as is well known, himself authored a now-lost treatise on fencing. If this work is ever rediscovered, we should not be surprised to find a link between the Milanese architect's work and that of one of the fathers of modern science.

— but a thrust, even of only two inches, is generally mortal, as it penetrates whatever vital part it is plunged into. Furthermore, when one strikes with a cut, the right arm and side are exposed, but a thrust can be made with the body covered and the adversary can be hit before he sees the blow. Therefore the Romans generally used this method in fighting. The reason they used wooden training swords and shields of double weight was that by becoming used to the greater weight, they could fight more securely and quickly.

93. Altoni, 67.

94. Albeit one clearly based on the illustrations of human proportions that accompany Cesariano's Italian translation of Vitruvius (q.v.).

95. Altoni, in chap. 11 of his work, describes something similar, but, again, his work likely never progressed beyond the manuscript.

Agrippa was hardly the first to apply mathematics to bodies in conflict. In the court of Urbino, "pure" mathematicians and geometers such as the "father of accounting" Luca Pacioli (1445–1514) and Piero della Francesca (1410–1514), whose mathematical studies of perspective recall the studies in the Codex Hyugens, worked alongside "practical" men such as the sculptor-architect Francesco di Giorgio Martini (1439–1508); Roberto Valturio (1405–75), author of the 1455 *De re militari*, which improved on Vegetius with technical diagrams; and the father-and-son architect-artists Girolamo Genga (1476–1551) and Bartolomeo (1518–58), who was commissioned to design the fortifications of Malta. Perhaps influenced by their work — or seeking to appeal to his employers' tastes — Vadi wrote that fencing, like music, is a science, arguing that the sword is subject to geometry:

> Geometry divides and separates
> with infinite numbers and measures
> that fill pages with knowledge.
> The sword is under its purview
> since it is useful to measure blows and steps
> in order to make the science more secure.
> Fencing is born from geometry....[96]

However, working as he was within a late-medieval pedagogical structure that stressed imitation of models over elucidation of theoretical fundamentals, Vadi did not greatly elaborate.

Likewise, the Venetian Niccolo Tartaglia (1499–1557), in his *La Nuova Scienza* (1537), had attempted to improve on medieval impetus theory by inventing an empirical science of ballistics by loading cannon with identical shot and equal charges and firing them at varying angles. However, this was a comparatively simple experiment. Agrippa attempted something much more difficult than merely predicting the flight of a cannon ball or depicting an inert body on canvas or stone: to scientifically break down the seemingly random motions of the body in time and space and reconstruct them into an intelligible vocabulary.

---

96. Folio 3v–4r.

All possible actions are analyzed and systematized into a learnable repertoire of techniques. In doing so, besides successfully combining his time's two dominant strains of mathematics, the practical and the courtly, Agrippa became perhaps history's first practitioner of kinesthology. Thus the metaphor of the geometrical diagram that appears beside the various figures in the first chapters of the book. Agrippa explains that, just as a stick taken rough from a tree is suitable for a skilled hand to draw any number of figures, such as squares, triangles, circles, hexagrams, etc., so too is the human body by its own nature a facile instrument to perform any of the actions necessary for fencing — therefore let not anyone complain that they are unsuited to learn this skill, for "a man, governing himself with reason and art, ought to do well in this pursuit."[97] Paralleling his other interests, Agrippa considered the human body geometrically as an inherently apt object.[98] "As with Leonardo Da Vinci, but also as with the commentators on Vitruvius and the artists of his time, [Agrippa] praises a metaphysic supposing the existence of an ideal proportion and a perfect action," as Briost, Drévillon, and Serna have put it — though the simple efficacy of Agrippa's art prohibits such an easy dismissal of its "metaphysical" groundings.[99] In fact, the macrocosmic implications of this "metaphysical" thread of reasoning are continued throughout the rest of the book and provide a key insight not only into Agrippa's worldview, but also into his system of fencing, for he was fond of couching practical fencing instruction in literate prose. For instance, in 1.11, having explained the actions at the core of his art and the simple actions derived from them, Agrippa introduces the following sequence of attacks and counters:

> ...move your left foot up against the right, make an attack to the enemy's outside — that is to the right side of his

---

97. I, 4.

98. Briost, Drévillon, and Serna, on pp. 145–46, hold that "the sides of the geometrical diagrams represent the different possible positions of the blade." Though their analysis of Agrippa's intellectual background is for the most part accurate, the authors are incorrect in this.

99. Briost, Drévillon, and Serna, pp. 144–45.

body — and send your sword over his by *forza*. If he parries, disengage quickly, stepping with your right foot towards his left side,[100] and, voiding your *vita*,[101] move your left foot to hit him in high Fourth. This is seen in the following figure, which has lines drawn from the two points of the eyes to its back to demonstrate that the eyes, although they are two, can not look in more than one place at a time. Nor do they naturally travel in parallel lines, but rather finish in only one point, like a pyramid.

Though, to someone unfamiliar with fencing theory this can seem mystifying at first, despite the seeming incongruity, all Agrippa is doing here (besides showing off his learning) is using the science of perspective to explain a fencing technique. Just like the visual rays cast from the eyes,[102] the opposing sword, traveling in a straight line, is considered geometrically. The evasive action that Agrippa explains is merely moving off what later schools called "the line of direction," a common principle in many later treatises.

Returning to the Vitruvian theme, in the twenty-fourth chapter of the first part we find another apparently perplexing object: in the undifferentiated space next to the figure is placed a ball. As Agrippa explains, though:

---

100. It is the step that frees the swords from the engagement or "cross."

101. *Vita* literally means "waist" but carries the connotation of "center of mass" (as in the Japanese *hara*) or "life." Agrippa is instructing us to void or twist our center of mass away from the oncoming point, as in the later *volte* of the French school. In the milieu of sixteenth-century Rome, such an action would inevitably recall the aesthetic ideal of *contrapposto* derived from Myron's Discobolos and the Belvedere Torso, and which is so well displayed in the figures on the Sistine ceiling, as well as Aristotle's view of rotation as the primary form of locomotion (*Physics* VIII, 9). For all of these reasons and connotations — the martial, the art-historical, and the metaphorical — we have thus left *vita* untranslated.

102. The Galenic "eye-spirit," a concept that goes back to Plato, but which was best expressed in Agrippa's time by Leonardo's and Alberti's writings on perspective. Alberti considered perspective monocularly; Leonardo, like Agrippa, binocularly.

...If you were to place the ball on the ground and try to strike it however you can, on whatever side you might wish to, you can well imagine that you will not be able to strike it firmly, no matter whether you hit it in the center or on the edge. This is because it defends itself with its motion. In fact, if you study how it moves, you will see that it is a naturally mobile instrument.

It therefore seems to me that this is a model of our bodies, which are not like balls insomuch concerning what they are made of, but rather in how they move. You can understand everything you need to know to use the techniques I have discussed if you remember that our bodies are the same as the ball and move with the same skill and agility....

While this can be seen as a simple example to express how one should move in offense and defense, Agrippa's ball hearkens back not only to the geometrical figure in the section on the lunge, but to Aristophanes' speech on the androgynes in the *Symposium* and, most importantly, Vitruvius' circular conception of the human body.[103] As Vitruvius says in *De Architectura* III.1 and 3 (loosely translated):

The composition of a temple whose rule the dutiful architect ought to observe comes from proportion, which is called *analog* in Greek. The proportion in all works comes from the harmony of all the parts, and from the ratio thereof comes symmetry. For there can be no temple without symmetry and proportion composed according to the proper rule, unless it has the exact proportion of man.... [Vitruvius goes on to give the proportions.]

Similar to how the parts of a sacred temple should be in accordance with the measure of the whole universe, parts should be in accordance with the whole. Again, the navel is the natural center of the body. Therefore, if a man lies

---

103. And lest we forget, Agrippa claimed association with Antonio Sangallo and Michelangelo, who were successively charged with the construction of St. Peter's, which Sangallo's teacher Bramante had originally conceived along Vitruvian lines.

down spread-armed and splay-footed, his hands and feet will describe a circle with its center in its navel, with his fingers and feet touching the circumference.

Agrippa's use of language also recalls one of the consul's lines from Alberti's *Anuli* ("rings"), one of the *Intercenales*: "Nothing is more capacious [than a cricle], nothing more whole in itself, nothing stronger, nothing more able to shrug off shattering blows because of its angles, nothing freer in its motion. Therefore, we must remain within the circle of reason, that is of humanity, which is connected and complicit with virtue, and God to virtue, which comes from God."[104] The difficulty with this interpretation is that *Anuli* was not published, let alone translated into the vernacular, until well after Agrippa wrote. However, it is not impossible that one of his compatriots had access to one of the two known manuscripts of *Anuli* (Vatican Ottoboniano 1424 and the Bibliothèque Nationale Lat. 6702), especially since the latter was likely in the possession Cardinal Niccolò Ridolfi (d. 1550 in Rome), before finding its way to the Bibliothèque du Roi. Certainly his sentiment is the same as Alberti's.

Human beings, then, are not only the mirrors of the universe, but naturally spherical, perfect, and capable of the seventh, primary, and most perfect form of Aristotelian motion, rotation about a center — in other words, we are models of the cosmos.[105] By one's own bodily nature one therefore ought to be able to execute all the required actions for offense and defense. A true heir to the Neoplatonic tradition of Pico della Mirandola and Ficino, Agrippa believes the human organism to be naturally perfect. This conception will be further detailed below in the explanation of Agrippa's idea of the *vita*.

In the second part of his treatise, Agrippa introduces more complicated actions, illustrated by pairs of fencers. These figures

---

104. *Leonis Baptistæ Alberti opera inedita*, ed. by Girolamo Mancini (Florence: J.C. Sansoni, 1890), 232.
105. *Physics* VIII, 9.

do not depict combats of two on two, as has been sometimes been misapprehended,[106] but rather sequences of actions that demonstrate fencing techniques *in time* — at the beginning and end of a sequence of actions. In doing so, Agrippa created a sort of time/motion study that anticipated the photography of Eadweard Muybridge, Duchamp's *Nude Descending a Staircase*, and the Gilbreths' therbligs by three hundred years.[107] Nonetheless, one might perhaps argue that, in contrast to the first section, the sequences of actions Agrippa shows in this part of the treatise are sometimes a bit *too* attenuated, favoring style over substance — or sound fencing sense.

Finally, in the third section of his work, Agrippa gives us the dialogue between himself and Annibale in which he further expounds upon the geometrical figure. This dialogue takes place over the course of three days. The first day's dialogue concerns geometry, specifically the figures of plane geometry that appeared alongside the four guards in the first part of the work. Explaining to Annibale how to make these figures, Agrippa first draws a circle, then, by moving the stick in equal increments around the perimeter, forms a hexagon; then, by connecting every other angle, a triangle. A square on the circumference is made by intersecting a line with the hexagon. A second square is then made, and then

---

106. See, for instance, Egerton Castle, *Schools and Masters of Fencing* (Mineola, NY: Dover Publications, 2003), 48 (originally published in 1885 as *Schools and Masters of Fence*) and Levi, *Bibliografia generale della scherma* (Florence: Luigi Niccolai, 1890), 10. (Gelli does not make the same error in later works.)

107. These double figures also show just how much scientific thought and the idea of illustration as a mimesis of chronological reality has permeated the minds of his contemporaries. A century or so prior to Agrippa's time, viewers would have taken it for granted that a picture could represent the same person at two different moments. Interestingly, some of the first actions analyzed with instantaneous photography were lunging fencers — see Muybridge's *Fencing (Mr. Bonifon and Mr. Austin)*, plate 349 from the series *Animal Locomotion* taken on 11 October 1885 and printed by the Photo-Gravure Company, New York, for the University of Pennsylvania, 1887, now at the Iris and B. Gerald Cantor Center for Visual Arts at Stanford University.

an octagon. Finally, from the intersections of the squares and the triangles, Agrippa makes a pentagon. This, needless to say, not only resembles the designs of the Palazzo Farnese and of St. Peter's, but is extraordinarily similar to the illustrations that accompany Cesarino's translation of Vitruvius' third book, which begins with the discussion of how the ideal human body describes a circle and how to go from there to measuring the figure's outstretched limbs to form a square.

On the second day, Agrippa returns *chez Annibale* to teach his friend the method of making an oval from an octagon and the "widest possible implication" of what they had previously discussed. He first compares the universe to an octagon inscribed in a circle and states that, while the Ptolemaic universe rotates on axes that run through its poles, the poles must not be considered physical objects, but loci around which the heavenly spheres, set in motion by the Infinite Power, rotate around their center.[108] The spheres of the seven planets move about like this because the universe, "by turning through the warm zone, scattered the seven planets, as I have said, which, though attracted to the center, cannot descend because of the concavity of their spheres. They relate to the eighth [and outermost] sphere itself, and travel on this route they have taken around the equator, because of their heaviness, avoiding the lighter regions, like the four temperate and the frigid zones."

While this again links Cesarino's Vitruvius and Cardinal Alessandro's lifelong concerns with astrological symbolism (for instance, the ceilings of the Sala della Cosmografia and the Sala del Mappamondo at Caprarola and the Farnese Atlas), Agrippa goes on to state that each sphere's poles (that is, the axis about which it rotates) are not all in the same spot, but rather each has them fixed differently, and that each planet goes in its separate course (that is to say, an elliptical path), because the spheres, far from being subtle bodies, "are heavy." In other words, because of their mass the planets travel in their routes.

---

108. Again, note Agrippa's use of the seventh form of Aristotelian motion, as well as his notion of a mechanistic universe ruled by a transcendent Deity.

The third day of the dialogue is the most significant, however, for it is in this portion of the dialogue that Camillo explains to Annibale that the Earth is *not* the center of the universe, as Aristotle intimates in the *Physics* and as Ptolemy states in the fifth chapter of the first book of the *Algamest*, but rather has a center in itself about which it rotates and the universe another. This revolutionary idea was unfortunately eclipsed by Copernicus' rather better-documented and more accurate *De revolutionibus orbium coelestium* published in 1543, though the latter was still not widely accepted.[109] Agrippa then goes on to prove his idea by showing how a star marked on the horizontal Arctic in winter will seem to move or disappear in the summer, which we now know to be so because the axis upon which the earth rotates is tilted.

Agrippa's explanation for this phenomenon is ultimately derived from the fourteenth-century natural philosophy of Nicole Oresme and Jean Buridan: parts of the earth ascend or descend as they get lighter or heavier during the heating of the summer or cooling of the winter. Nonetheless, there was evidently a strong demand for Ptolemaic explanations, and so Blado's heirs republished the dialogue independently in 1575 as *Modo da comporre il moto nella sfera.*[110]

---

109. On Copernius' reception, see Owen Gingerich, *The Book Nobody Read* (New York: Walker & Company, 2004). Agrippa's cosmological system, it should be noted, also parallels his fencing: one voids the *vita*, the center, taking it off the axis of the enemy's attack.

110. For an excellent discussion of late medieval cosmology, see Edward Grant, *Planets, Stars, and Orbs: The Medieval Cosmos 1200–1687* (Cambridge: Cambridge University Press, 1994), 622–24. Oresme discusses this in his *Quaestiones de sphaera*, edited and translated by Garrett Droppers as "The Quaestiones de spera [sic] of Nicholas Oresme" (Ph.D dissertation, University of Wisconsin-Madison, 1966). For Buridan, see *Questiones super libros quattuor de caelo et mundo*, ed. by E. A. Moody (Cambridge, MA: Medieval Academy of America, 1942), 266. A fascinating commonality between Oresme and Agrippa is their mutual fascination with bodies in motion in time; this, and the intellectual tradition connecting Oresme and the Farnese circle, is fertile ground for further research. Oreseme's influence is also clearly shown in Agrippa's works on natural philosophy.

Many have wondered about the place of a dialogue on astronomy in a fencing work. The Victorian fencing antiquarian Egerton Castle apparently did not even bother to read it, remarking immediately after his rather positivist comment on Agrippa being "much in advance of the popular notions of his days" that "[a]s an engineer he studied the link movements performed by the various parts of the human anatomy in the actions of thrusting and cutting, and his mathematical mind revelled in geometrical figures and optical diagrams devised for their explanation. No doubt his 'philosophical dialogue' on that subject is very tedious...."[111] However, within the context of the work as a whole, the dialogue makes eminent sense. The classical *quadrivium* can be seen as the study of number — arithmetic as pure number, geometry as number in space, music as number in time, and astronomy, like fencing, as number in time and space. Agrippa thus seeks to show that his understanding of Euclid's geometry and Aristotle's ideas of motion and time are superior to that of the medieval consensus, just as his fencing knowledge, likewise derived from first principles, is superior to that of the traditional schools.[112]

The educated observer would have likewise observed a kinship between Agrippa's diagram of the universe and the cosmological diagrams accompanying Cesariano's 1521 translation of Vitruvius. As Raphael's grouping of geometry, astromomy, and geography together in the Stanza della Signatura in the Vatican shows, these were considered to be intimately related arts. Finally, also note here how Agrippa uses a combination of inductive observation of nature and reconciliation with traditional deductive authority. The scientific revolution did not take place by the survival of the

---

111. Castle, 45

112. I see no evidence that, as Briost, Drévillon, and Serna maintain, Agrippa attempted to further the question of acceleration and non-uniform movements as discussed by such Scholastics as Oresme (p. 146); rather, his conceptions are only derived therefrom. *Modo di compone il moto nell sfera* was, again, a reprint of his astronomical dialogue (the implications of which will be discussed below), and not an attempt to re-open this Scholastic debate.

fittest idea, but arose as one meme more successfully reproduced itself in the sixteenth-century politico-intellectual environment.

Moreover, Agrippa's cosmological schema has metaphysical implications. Human beings are the image of, and the center of, the (Ptolemaic) universe. Just as the stick is sufficient to draw all the geometrical figures, which in turn give us the principles for finding out the structure of the universe, the human body, that is the proportional mirror of the universe, is good enough to execute all the necessary actions of fencing. The legible — which is to say, the trainable — body is a mirror of the cosmos; one who fences according to natural principles is in alignment with the will of a transcendent Creator.

While all of this would have resonated with the educated contemporary, it also had real martial aplication. Exactly how Euclid's ideas of geometry and Aristotle's ideas of motion in time are applied in Agrippa's fencing will be seen in the following section.

AGRIPPA'S FENCING PRINCIPLES

Fundamental to understanding Agrippa's system of fencing is his idea of time, and key to Agrippa's idea of time is Aristotle's explanation of the subject in the *Physics*.[113] To Aristotle, time is "number of motion in respect to the before and after" *(tempus est numerus motus secundum prius et posterius)*, and throughout the Middle Ages, Scholastic philosophers insisted that time can only be known in relation to moving things.[114] Similarly, to Agrippa, a *tempo*, or

---

113. Thanks to Bob Charron for originally pointing out to me the relationship between Aristotelian physics and fencing time in his explication of Fiore dei Liberi at the Kalamazoo Medieval Congress in 2005.

114. Physics IV.11. On the Scholastics, see Milic Capek, "The Conflict between the Absolutist and the Relational Theory of Time before Newton," *Journal of the History of Ideas* 48.4 (Oct. 1987): 595–608; Richard C. Dales, "Time and Eternity in the Thirteenth Century," *Journal of the History of Ideas* 49.1 (Jan. 1988): 27–45; and Dirk-Jan Dekker, "Buridan's Concept of Time, Motion and the Soul in John Buridan's *Questions on Aristotle's Physics*"

"time," is *not* quantifiable in terms of the Newtonian absolute, abstract clock-time we have become accustomed to, but is a *relative*, Aristotelian conception based on the various actions one makes in fencing. One *tempo*, simply put, is *the interval it takes to perform a single, simple fencing action.*[115] This action can be a step forwards or backwards, a simple parry, a shift of one's weight from one foot to another, an extension of the arm, or the *passo straordinario* Agrippa illustrates in I, 2. Conversely, a parry followed by a riposte — two discrete actions — would be two *tempi*.[116]

With the idea of time understood, we can see how Agrippa uses an Aristotelian vocabulary to show us when and how to move. For instance, in 2.3, he says that if two men are fighting, with one in the guard of C and the other in the guard of D, then while D is changing his guard — in other words, in the time he makes by moving — C should make a straight thrust to his chest, and that "this is called countertime in favor of C." The logic here is that while the adversary is making one action, such as changing his guard, he cannot perform another. Should the adversary, in turn, seek to defend himself, we must follow with a counteraction. Agrippa illustrates this, after discussing the elementary principles, in the sequences of actions in the second part of the treatise.

Thus, Agrippa's prohibition against parrying, as it gives time to the adversary, since again, parrying and then riposting are two motions, which by definition takes two times. Rather, Agrippa says to perform defenses at the *same time (medesimo tempo)* that the adversary attacks — in other words, to counterattack. For instance, in 1.4 he instructs, "If you want to defend against a cut to the arm,

in *The Metaphysics and Natural Philosophy of John Buridan*, ed. by Johannes M.M.H. Thijssen and Jack Zupko (Leiden: Brill, 2001), 151–63.

115. This definition is still followed today.

116. It must be mentioned that this Aristotelian conception of fencing time was hardly unique to Agrippa. Altoni says "time is nothing more than the space of motion" (*il tempo non è altro che spatio di moto*, p. 76), and Altoni, Vadi, and the Bolognese writers all make use of terms such as *mezzo tempo* and *doppio tempo*.

then in the same time the enemy makes the cut, turn your hand into Fourth, extend your arm, and make a thrust."[117]

In the same way, Agrippa says, if the adversary attempts to beat or dominate one's blade, one should counterattack in the same time by dipping one's point beneath the opposing steel (so that he meets nothing but air) while extending one's arm and making a thrust. Later Italian writers would call the technique of not allowing the contact *cavare*, to "give way" or "make a vacuum," and, as we mentioned above, the Bolognese master Calvacabo[118] credits Agrippa with inventing it. We have chosen to translate this action contextually by the modern English fencing terms "disengage" and "deceive," particularly when Agrippa uses shorthand such as "escape" *(schiffare)* or "turn underneath the opposing sword's guard" *(girandola di sotto il fornimento de la spada contraria),* since this is, essentially, the action he is describing.

Agrippa's body mechanics are designed to enable his student to efficiently and spontaneously use time and its corollary, distance (since, after all, distance is rate multiplied by time). We have already seen how Agrippa held with the straight thrust as the quickest and most efficacious means of attacking, and accordingly disagrees with the practice of going on guard with the sword cocked over the shoulder. Even less does he hold with going on guard with the left foot forwards; save for certain necessary circumstances, his

---

117. Again, this is nothing new, but similar to the *mezzo tempo,* or "half time," mentioned by Vadi and Altoni and also by later writers such as Capo Ferro, in which an adversary's attack is interrupted with a quicker action — preferably in a manner that leaves one defended! Conversely, Manciolino says to parry and then follow with a riposte, which is two times — one to defend, and one to counterattack (p. 6).

This idea also raises the legal issue of the plaintiff in a judicial duel having the right to strike first: how does one reconcile this with a thrust in *medesimo tempo?*

118. His treatise is best known to us from a French translation of his Italian manuscript. Briost, Drévillon, and Serna (p. 66, n. 1) note that the translation of Calvacabo's manuscript (BnF MS Italien 1527) was made by the seigneur de Villamont and was published in Boven in 1597.

footwork has us always keep our dominant sword-side forwards (albeit not always as profiled as later writers would have it). In 1.2 he speaks of "half-," "ordinary" and "forced" (or "extraordinary") steps. The half-step *(mezzo passo, o'l passo)* is simply moving one foot forwards in a sort of demi-lunge. The "ordinary" step "taken all together" *(intero ordinario)* seems to be a longer step with the front foot. The *passo sforzato* or *straordinario* is similar to the lunge. We cannot speak definitively of Agripa's mechanics, but in the classical or modern lunge, the impetus for the attack comes not from launching the body forwards (thus making it difficult to re-cover to safety) but from the rear foot pushing against the ground. Sometimes Agrippa's feet are spaced widely apart (for instance, after making the "extraordinary step"), and sometimes narrowly, depending on the exigencies of the situation; by moving the rear leg up to the front, he can gain distance on the attack, and by pulling his front leg back, he can pull his torso out of the enemy's reach.

Most importantly, the fencer is never double-weighted but rather maintains his center of gravity over either one foot or the other, so that, like the ball, he can move naturally and spontaneously in any direction. Agrippa elucidates this in 1.24 in the course of explaining a counteroffensive action.[119]

The keys to this technique are two important concepts: the idea of *forza*, and the idea of the *vita. Forza* is, simply, the mechani-cal action of one sword on another. Many times in his treatise, Agrippa instructs us to touch the opposing sword with one's own and attack by *forza* — literally, "strength," but here used in the sense of the leverage of the "strong" part of the sword, that with the most mechanical advantage, which is to say the part nearest the hilt against the weaker part of the adversary's weapon, that nearer the point. By choosing the right time to place the blade in the position where it will simultaneously exert the maximum leverage and keep the adversary's blade under control, one's own sword acts as a barrier between one's body and the opposing steel — "attacking with opposition" while "closing the line" in fencing

---

119. See pp. 50–54 below.

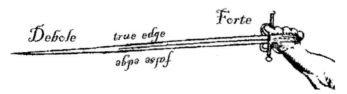

Fig. 2. Parts of the Sword.

parlance. This is not a new idea (it arguably appears in 1.33, and Altoni also discusses "all the ways one sword can move against the other"), but Agrippa employs the principle with a high degree of refinement and subtlety.

Furthermore, though Agrippa advises us to keep our eyes on the enemy's hand, the real cue for making actions in countertime is the touch of steel on steel. For instance, in 1.11, he tells us, "make an attack to the enemy's outside — that is to the right side of his body — and send your sword over his by *forza*. If he disengages or deceives your attampt to engage, counter-disengage quickly, stepping with your right foot towards his left side, and, voiding your *vita*, move your left foot to hit him in high Fourth." What is important to understand (and what Agrippa leaves unsaid) is that the stimulus is not, and cannot be, perceived by the eyes. It must be felt by touch. The subconscious mind registers the subtle pressure of blade on blade via the central nervous system before the conscious mind does, allowing an exponentially quicker response. The same applies to any situation where one touches ("engages") the opposing sword: by engaging the adversary's steel with one's own, one can easily ascertain his disposition and intentions.

These techniques, however, are not easy; they requires as much sensitivity and *buone maniere* (to borrow Vasari's term) as wielding a paintbrush. The sword became an instrument not of cleverness or workmanlike skill, but of genius. Conversely, in II, 25, Agrippa does not favor the two-handed sword "because of the uncertain rules that govern its blows, which travel so through the air" — thus obviating the principles of *forza*.

Likewise, in all his multifarious evasions, Agrippa frequently says that one should *fuggir* — "escape," "flee," or, better yet, "void" — one's *vita*. This bears some explanation. *Vita* means "waist" in modern Italian, but Florio, writing in 1611, gives the translation as "life, spirit, naturall vigour, any body's manner of life. Also, forme, fashion, or maner of living. Used also for the stature or proportion of man or woman," but Agrippa's use of the word was more multifarious than even this plethora of meaning suggests.[120] By examining the way *vita* is used in technical treatises on fencing and dancing, we can gain a more complete idea of the way early modern Italians thought of their bodies and their sense of corporeal aesthetics, as well as the shift in the word's meaning between the seventeenth century and today.

For instance, Fabritio Caroso, in his *Il Ballarino* (1581) makes reference to *vita civile* and honest pleasures as necessary to the *conservatione di…vita*,[121] but also the *vita* as something that can be ornamented by dancing the *fioretto* agilely on the ball of one's foot,[122] something that we must turn to the left and push a little forwards without raising the left foot in order to perform the steps of a galliard (*cinque passi soprapiede in Gagliarda*),[123] something we must carry properly in order to make the jumping step known as a *capriole*, something we turn a little to the left and then a little to the right in the dance known as *amor felice*,[124] and something we turn to our lady partners after bowing at the end of the *contrapasso nuovo*.[125] Later, in his *Nobilità di Dame* (1600), Caroso also uses *vita* as synonymous with "life," but also, in his instructions on how to bow, has the master tell his disciple to "…move your leg backwards,

---

120. Florio, 603 col. 3.

121. In the dedication and missive the reader, respectively. See the transcription and facsimile by Greg Lindahl (available at http://www.pbm.com/~lindahl/caroso/, (accessed Apr. 7, 2007).)

122. Caroso (1581), Book I, Regola XXVI.

123. Caroso (1581), Book I, Regola XXXI.

124. Caroso (1581), Book II, 92.

125. Caroso (1581), Book II, 148.

move your *vita* a little backwards, straighten your knee some...."[126] Similarly, Negri, in his 1604 dance manual *Nuove inventioni di balli* ("in which are shown the proper ways to carry the *vita* and comport oneself with graceful movements to the manners and grace of Love"),[127] describes how some people let their *vita* fall clumsily over one foot and then the other when walking in the street, but elegant people ought to move *from* the *vita* with moderate, balanced steps.

We can thus see the multifarious meanings one word might have — the *vita* is at once the source of bodily energy, the physical center, both in terms of center of mass and middle of a man's measure — and life itself. What Agrippa is instructing us to do by *fuggir la vita*, then, is void or twist our center of mass away from the oncoming point. In the milieu of sixteenth-century Rome, such an action would inevitably recall the navel as the center of the Vitruvian figure, as well as the aesthetic ideal of *contrapposto* ultimately derived from Myron's Discobolos and the Belvedere Torso, and which is so well displayed in Salviati's painting and Michelangelo's figures on the Sistine ceiling. It is also, of course, Aristotle's view of rotation as the primary form of locomotion (*Physics* VIII, 9). The cosmological schema of the dialogue reflects this, as well. Just as the center of the Earth moves with respect to the center of the universe, so, too, can the fencer void his *vita* to escape the enemy's attack. We are, after all, images of the cosmos. This is Agrippa's great accomplishment. He has married *contrapposto* to the Vitruvian schema of the human body and the universe. We might as well say Mannerism was influenced by fencing as fencing by Mannerism. Read in the light of the conversations that must have taken place in sixteenth-century Rome, Adam's twisting posture on the Sistine ceiling, so reminscent of the Belvedere Torso, becomes a visual representation of the idea that man was created in God's image, which is to say that of the universe.

---

126. Transcription and facsimile by Greg Lindahl, available at http://www.pbm.com/~lindahl/negri/ (accessed Apr. 7, 2007).
127. The subtitle of the frontispiece.

But causes precede effects. The simple effectiveness of Agrippa's art is a rebuttal of Sydney Anglo's statements concerning the flawed application of mathematical analysis in fencing treatises. Professor Anglo says this was mistaken in three assumptions — "that analysis of movement is identical with its notation, whereas analysis follows rather than precedes an activity"; that "in order to perform any movement effectively, it is necessary to understand the scientific principles underlying it"; and that "[masters] fundamentally misunderstood the real nature of the movements they sought to notate" regarding "fencing as a kind of dance."[128]

In the first case, Agrippa makes it clear that empirical observation and experience precedes theory; in the second, he uses geometry and physics as pedagogical devices to, respectively, *illustrate* and *analyze* the most efficient ways for bodies in combat to move; and in the third, fencing time is unlike dancing, for, while both involve the Aristotelian relativistic conception of time as "the number of stillness and motion," in a dance we expect regularity and predictability from the music, whereas in fencing we base our time on the irregular and unpredictable actions of the adversary. For all its ornament, Agrippa's schema of fencing remains not only similar to what had gone before, but also quite effective; it is only that the principles are explained in the idiom of the educated courtier. It is this quality that no doubt contributed to his lasting success.

AGRIPPA'S SENSE OF AESTHETICS

Anglo also likens rapier fence to commando-style "all-in fighting," stating that "Renaissance duels and armed affrays were analogous to war; and, to judge from the homicidal pages of the masters and the bloodstained record of personal combats, prisoners were rarely taken."[129] This statement may be taken as a précis of one of Professor Anglo's main theses, but it is one with which I must

---

128. Sydney Anglo, *The Martial Arts of Renaissance Europe* (New Haven: Yale University Press, 2000), 63.
129. *Martial Arts*, 273.

disagree. Rather, I would prefer Van Orden's conceptualization. To her, all three performatives were intimately related, sharing a common aesthetic vocabulary.[130] This is not the same as saying that fencing was in any way choreographed, but rather, just as any other cultural form — particularly one that was a performance of class — that it was subject to social dicta.

Using a sword in public, be it in a friendly bout or a duel is, lest we forget, a performance of sorts, and, at least in theory, certain rules applied. As Muir has summarized, "courtliness erected rigid barriers between the human and the animal, condemning all animal-like behavior in men and women.... Thus good manners repressed emotions. The courteous denied or delayed all impulses, never admitted fear, controlled and channeled anger into the duel, and sublimated sexual appetites through elaborate flirtations."[131] Those who did not cut a *bella figura* on the battlefield could face ridicule. Castiglione has Count Ludovico denounce those cowards who, like the cousins of Ancona, display a lack of class and become laughing-stocks by "wasting time debating every point of the rules, choosing weapons that can neither cut nor thrust, arming themselves as for artillery barrages, and, thinking it enough not to be defeated, are always standing on the defensive and retreating."[132]

Agrippa's *scienza di scherma* was eminently well-suited to this new form of masculine martialism, for it was grounded in aesthetics, as well as science. What were these aesthetic principles? Agrippa is unabashedly Mannerist in his tastes, favoring fluid, graceful, circular motion, the human body twisting about its center, and actions that tend to elongate the body. Whether this is the exaggerated Mannerist posting of a Pontormo, a Giulio Romano, a Parmigianino, or a Bronzino, is, of course, debatable, but studying Agrippa's combative principles invites us to look at sixteenth-century depictions of bodies in motion a new light. This was *not*

---

130. See n. 24 above.
131. Muir, 163–64.
132. *Libro del Cortegiano*, 76 (I, 21).

form without function, however, and certainly Agrippa's system is still a practical method of swordsmanship.

Likewise Agrippa favors brains over brawn; the instructions he gives are many times explicitly for the benefit of the "smaller man." Castiglione, after all, prefers his courtier to be short and athletic rather than big and burly, since, as Count Ludovico says, "many times those who are larger in body, besides being dull of mind, are inapt at the sorts of agile exercises I wish the courtier to undertake."[133]

In all, Agrippa's ideas concerning fencing are not only good martial sense, but a tangible demonstration of what Castiglione calls *sprezzatura*.[134] This *sprezzatura*, derived from Cicero's *dissimulatio*, is, as Jennifer Richards has argued, destabilizing to the idea of a nobility of blood, instead replacing it with a nobility of performance.[135] In the end, the nobility of the courtier was as much about acting the part as ancestry — and Agrippa's treatise after all shows us how to handle the preeminent symbol of the aristocracy, the sword. Furthermore, practice is essential to both *sprezzatura* and swordsmanship: one can only achieve true nonchalance or skill by continual repetition, until the actions become second nature.

The trick to *sprezzatura*, however, is concealing one's practice, making skill look effortless and natural. This brings us to the most telling instance of the courtier's cool-headedness — Agrippa's combative mindset. An art such as Agrippa's functions only when applied in a cool, detached manner. The untrained man, his flight-or-flight response flooding his system with adrenaline, is ruled by his natural instinct to beat the enemy's sword away, or to take

---

133. *Libro del Cortegiano* 76 (I, 20). The Italians may have also been aware of a disparity between themselves and the larger, heavier Germans. On the average height of men in the medieval and early modern periods, see Richard H. Steckel, "New Light on the 'Dark Ages': The Remarkably Tall Stature of Northern European Men during the Medieval Era," *Social Science History* 28.2 (Summer 2004): 211-28.

134. *Libro del Cortegiano* 81 (I, 26).

135. Jennifer Richards, "Assumed Simplicity and the Critique of Nobility: Or, How Castiglione Read Cicero," *Renaissance Quarterly* 54.2 (July 2001): 460–86.

enormous, powerful swings at his foe. This is far from the most efficient way to use a weapon. A timely, well-aimed thrust can end an argument with greater surety than the panicked actions of the *uomo bestiale* (to borrow the term used by Ridolfo Capo Ferro in 1610). Muir, in *Mad Blood Stirring*, may have described the savage vendetta killers of Friuli as imitating a dog-pack,[136] but martial-arts scholar and combat veteran Donn Draeger in his many works on Japanese *bujitsu*, and career military officer Dave Grossman in his seminal book *On Killing*, draw on another animal metaphor to explain the comportment of the trained man-at-arms — that of a cool, detached predator, the wolf instead of the dog.[137] This is likewise the aesthetic of courtly bloodshed: to always be in control of oneself, even when committing acts of raw violence. It is, hoplologically speaking, good advice: train the body — fashion the instrument — and it will perform many times better. As Archimedes is held to have said, "give me a lever and a place to stand, and I can move the world." Agrippa's art provides the lever; it requires, however, the power of the human mind to apply it. This is the meaning of the "reason and art" by which a man should govern himself: not merely observing the reasoned principles laid forth in the treatise, but remaining level-headed — in

---

136. "Through the mimetic process of modeling vendetta killing on hunting, killers exempted themselves from the normal responsibilities of normal mankind" (Muir, xxix).

137. See Donn F. Draeger and Robert W. Smith, *Asian Fighting Arts* (Tokyo: Kodansha International, 1969); Donn Draeger, *Classical Bujitsu* (New York: Weatherhill, 1973); Donn F. Draeger and Robert W. Smith, *Comprehensive Asian Fighting Arts* (Tokyo: Kodansha International, 1980); Gordon Warner and Donn F. Draeger, *Japanese Swordsmanship* (New York: Weatherhill, 1982), among others; and Lt. Col. Dave Grossman, *On Killing: The Psychological Cost of Learning to Kill in War and Society* (Boston: Little Brown, 1996). See also J. Christopher Amberger's writings on mensur, dueling, and fear in his *Secret History of the Sword* (Baltimore: Hammerterz Verlag, 1999); the fine essays on Diane Skoss' Koryu Books Web site, www.koryu.com; and Hunter B. Armstrong's writings on the web site of the International Hoplology Society at http://www.hoplology.com.

command of one's intellect — when the time came to use it. This may not have always been the case in practice, but it was certainly the performative ideal.

Such performance, however, required much rehearsal. Or, as Vincent Saviolo, one of the Italian masters — whom George Silver so hated — who had come to London to teach rapier put it in his 1595 book *His Practice*:

> I advise you to exercise your selfe in all these points I have set down unto you, because besides the knowledge, you shall make your practise absolute in such sorte that when occasion to serve to speake of such matters, you maie be able to give a sufficient reason therof, & also defend your selfe against such as will offer you injurie, for the worlde is nowe subject to many wronges and insolencies. But you shall thereby make your self most perfect, and how far more in this behalf then I have uttered unto you, for it is not possible in this art to express all by words, which by your own experience and diversity of occurrences you shall find.[138]

Saviolo's words bring us to the last point on this subject: fencing — the practice of the art of the sword — is not identical with dueling. Even if the term *fioretto*, signifying the nail-headed foil used in rapier fencing, cannot be documented in the Italian language until 1598, this does mean the object itself did not exist. The Royal Armouries in Leeds, for instance, has on display a fencing rapier with a quadrangular blade and a nail-headed point dated to 1580. It is in all respects, save the swept hilt, similar to an Italian fencing foil from c. 1880 displayed in the next case. This object is a testament not only to the fact that gentleman were training in Agrippa's thrust-oriented art within a generation of his writing, but also, as is confirmed by the distinctions between fencing for amusement and fencing for one's life made by Agrippa's successors such as Giacomo di Grassi, Vincent Saviolo, and Ridolfo Capo Ferro, that

---

138. Vincent Saviolo, *His Practice* (London, 1595).

the applications thereof were not all on the dueling-ground.[139] Such masters maintain that in fencing with such relatively safe practice weapons, either for amusement and training, one may feint with impunity and thus show one's brilliance and skill; on the field of battle, one opens oneself up to a deadly counterthrust.[140] Yet, there was no doubt that such gentlemanly amusements were widespread: fencing, as J.C.F. Marshall points out, was part of training in "courtesy," one accomplishment among many. Dueling was only the extreme edge of the custom of bearing arms.[141] For what was no doubt the majority of European gentlemen, the closest experience of arms was the give-and-take and sense of mutual respect and courtesy imparted by foil play in the fencing salle. In the end, the largest lesson of the *salle d'armes* is not how to kill, but how to live.

AGRIPPA AND HERMETICISM

In addition to Euclid's geometry, Vitruvius' architecture and Aristotle's ideas of time, Agrippa's method of fencing arguably incorporates Pythagorean ideas reintroduced by Ficino's reading of Iamblichus' *On Pythagoreanism* and Michael Psellos' paraphrases thereof. The difficulty is that, just as he does not mention Vitruvius, Agrippa does not cite hermetic works, or indeed any authorities other than Euclid and Aristotle; the closest he comes to explicitly mentioning Ficino is his dedication to Cosimo I, in which he evokes the memory of the duke of Florence's ancestors, patrons of Marsilio Ficino and of Pico della Mirandola: "Because

---

139. Incidentally, it is also a material witness to the fact that Italian fencing used essentially the same weapon and the same principles for hundreds of years.

140. I say "relatively safe" advisedly; masks were not worn and the loss of eyes in practice was not uncommon.

141. This point is made by Marshall in her unpublished work, presented as a paper entitled "'Come and See the Violence Inherent in the System'? The Multifarious Nature of Elizabethan and Jacobean Rapier Fencing," at the Renaissance Society of America Fifty-Third Annual Meeting (Miami, FL, Aug. 22–24, 2007).

the world knows that your most worthy ancestors were true restorers of good letters, and good studies of science, and of valuable
languages, and you, accompanying arms with letters, are the true
sustainer of letters and of arms, it appears right to me to consecrate
this, my work, to the Your Excellency's most renowned name."
Yet, as Christopher S. Celenza, after identifying the sources used
by one's subject, "One must imagine internally coherent modes of
thinking into which a thinker could have tapped and sketched social
context in which he could have imagined and in which he might
have imagined himself."[142] In the absence of definite documentary
proof, we must argue for Agrippa's Pythagorean connection from
the internal evidence of the work itself, and from what it meant
to the self-made early modern gentleman.

For instance, why are there four principal guards, as opposed
to the twelve favored by Marozzo or the three later endorsed by
other masters? "These are the Principals," Agrippa tells us, "because
from them proceed and are formed many other guards according
to the necessary considerations and occurrences of this exercise."
Four is, also, of course, a number of hermetic significance, since it
is the *tetractys*, containing within itself all other numbers: $1 + 2 +$
$3 + 4$ is 10.[143] From these primary positions, Agrippa tells us, we
can derive any of the infinitely varied other actions we might need
in the course of the exercise. And, indeed, he gives us ten other
positions, identified by the letters E through P (omitting M and J,
which in alphabets at this time is the same as I).

This is additionally seen in the allegorical scene preceding
the dialogue. The dialogue begins with Annibale coming to visit
Agrippa and begging him not to publish the treatise without explaining the geometrical figures "since they can confuse the readers
and might be understood otherwise than you intended." Camillo
replies that it is good that Annibale has come "because last night, I

142. Christopher Celenza, "Pythagoras in the Renaissance: The Case of
Marsilio Ficino," *Renaissance Quarterly* 52:3 (Autumn 1999): 667–711.
143. Aristotle references this in *De Anima*, I, 2. See S. K. Heninger, Jr., "Some
Renaissance Versions of the Pythagorean Tetrad," *Studies in the Renaissance*
8. (1961): 7–35.

had a vision of being attacked by certain philosophers. They were completely against my using the piece of wood to make those figures that you mentioned, or talking about certain other things.... Rather, they thought me presumptuous for wanting to discuss such matters without having studied them. After that, it seemed to me that I defended myself with the help of many gentlemen who were friends of mine." And, indeed, there are Agrippa's friends, hacking away at the philosophers with their angles.[144]

Fig. 3. Hieroglyphs.

In the engraving that illustrates this vision or dream, an obelisk appears behind Agrippa, set into a landscape of Roman ruins. This intriguing symbol is not explained in the text, but cannot help but recall the one in the Circus of Gaius and Nero that had preoccupied him since his arrival in Rome. More significantly, we find inscribed on the obelisk four hieroglyphics — three at the top, and one, over Agrippa's head, at the bottom. What might the meaning of this message be? Interpreting the symbols is difficult, since we must first determine what each one represents, and then what their combined meaning might be in the context of the sources available to Agrippa. The first symbol initially appears to be a serpent, signifying "one who vanquishes all" according to Horapollo's *Hieroglyphica*.[145] However, the Ferrari edition is not illustrated; if, though, we look to Bolzani's *Hieroglyphica* (published in 1556, three years after Agrippa's *Trattato*) for a visual cue, Agrippa's figure seems to be not a serpent, but an

---

144. Castle, 48–49, misunderstood this illustration, thinking that the various costumes represented Venetians and Romans vying to retain Agrippa's services or drag him away

145. *Dissegnono un Serpente intiero, come uogliono dare a intendere un uincitor d'ogni cosa.* An Italian version of John of Trebezond's Latin translation was produced by Pietro Vasolli and published as *Delli segni hierogliphici* by Gabriel Giolito de Ferrari (Venice, 1547), 1.64. Hypertext version at http://www.studiolum.com/en/cd08-horapollo.htm (accessed Apr. 10, 2007).)

eel, which, according to Bolzani, means either *prudentia* or — more likely — *odium* and *invidia*.[146] To Ferrari, however, the eel (*anguilla*) represents a "man who is enemy to all."[147] As Ferrari would have been available to Agrippa (and as there is no evidence that Agrippa himself knew Latin, since the classical sources he used would have been available in translation), it is to his interpretation we must defer, while using Bolzani as our reference to how contemporaries might have understood the iconography.

The remaining figures are somewhat easier to interpret. The second from the top is an eagle, recognizable from its powerful legs and hooked beak. Though the most well-known Farnese eagle is the one ridden by a thunderbolt-hurling Jupiter (identified by Caro as symbolic of the temporal power Paul III left his cardinal-grandson) and depicted on the ceiling fresco of the Sala del Mappamondo painted by Giovanni de'Vecchi in the 1570s, the device occurs also on a medal of Paul III by Alessandro Cesati (now in the National Gallery of Art, Washington, DC) showing Ganymede and a Jovian eagle.[148] To Horapollo, the eagle means God, exaltedness, excellence, blood, victory, or paradoxically, lowering.[149] The last two signs match images from Francesco Colonna's *Hypnerotomachia Poliphili*. The arrows, according to the

---

146. Giovanni Piero Valeriano Bolzani, *Hieroglyphica* (Basel, 1556).

147. Ferrari 2.103.

148. On the Cesati medal and Farnese Jovian imagery, see Stinger, 260–61. On Farnese iconography in Caprarola and Caro's hand in its design, see Loren Patridge's several works, especially "The Farnese Circular Courtyard in Caprarola: God, Geopolitics, Genealogy, and Gender," *The Art Bulletin* 83.2 (Jan. 2001): 259–93; "The Room of Maps at Caprarola, 1573–75," *The Art Bulletin* 77.3 (Sept. 1995): 413–44; and "Divinity and Dynasty at Caprarola: Perfect History in the Room of Farnese Deeds," *The Art Bulletin* 60.3 (Sept. 1978): 494–530. For more on Farnese astrology, see Mary Quinlan–McGrath, "Caprarola's Sala della Cosmografia," *Renaissance Quarterly* 50.4 (Winter 1997): 1045–1100. Caro's comment may be found on p. 144 of volume 1 of his *Lettere Familiare*, ed. by Aulo Greco (Florence: Le Monnier, 1961).

149. *Come vogliono dimostrare Iddio, overo altezza, o abbassamento, o excellenza, o sangue, o vittoria, dipingono un'Aquila.* Ferrari 1.6.

Hypnerotomachia, are *contraria et velocissima*.[150] The other bird at the base of the obelisk, over Agrippa's head, seems to most resemble a figure that the text of the *Hypnerotomachia* explains to be a goose (*ansere*),[151] which, according to the Ferrari edition (which uses the presumably Venetian dialect *chinalopia*), means "son."[152]

Therefore, we have a somewhat cryptic statement seemingly referring to the political situation, with a Farnese eagle set against an all-conquering (imperial?) serpent, or possibly against unsociable, hateful, envious Scholastic philosophers, who are opposed to the "Farnese-aligned "son," — that is, Agrippa — heir to the truth of the ancients, much as the supposedly Egyptian-derived *prisca theologia* of Hermes Trimegistus so occupied Ficino. This would rhyme well with the allegorical scene in the frontispiece. Much as with Peter Gay's conception of the Enlightenment as the revival of ancient philosophy (in this case, Lucretius' Epicureanism) melded with Newtonian natural philosophy,[153] Agrippa's authority is derived not from his overturning of centuries of thought in favor of observation from Nature, but from his empirical rediscovery of the principles along which even more ancient wisdom operated. Alternatively, we can see a Christian meaning — a Farnese God (the eagle) opposed to the serpent, with the "son" (Christ) in a lower, mundane register.

The dialogue itself is also rich with symbolism. The first day's conversation concerns geometry, specifically the figures that appeared alongside the four guards. Agrippa first draws a circle, symbolizing the world, then, by moving the stick in equal increments around the perimeter, forms a hexagon; then, by connecting every other angle, a triangle (symbolic, of course, of the Trinity). A square on the circumference is made by intersecting a line with the hexagon. A second square is then made, and then

---

150. *Hypnerotomachia*, 262
151. Francesco Colonna, *Hypnerotomachia Poliphili* (Venice, 1499), 41, http://mitpress.mit.edu/e-books/HP/hyp041.htm (accessed June 11, 2009).
152. Ferrari 1.53.
153. Peter Gay, *The Enlightenment: An Interpretation*, 2 vols. (New York: Random House, 1966–69; revised ed. New York: Norton, 1995).

an octagon. Finally, from the intersections of the squares and the triangles, Agrippa makes a pentagon — which, besides recalling the pentagonal Farnese palace in Caprarola with its circular courtyard — in Vitruvius, in Henry Cornelius Agrippa's *Three Books of Occult Philosophy*, and in Bolzani's *Heroglyphica*, is symbolic of health, Christ, and of the human body. Thus, we come full circle, so to speak: the human being is as the stick, which creates the circle, from which the pentagon is ultimately derived. This Vitruvian cosmological idea of the human body is fully realized, insofar as fencing goes at least, with Girard Thibault's treatise of 1628, in which he constructs an elaborate diagram intended to elucidate the distance and proportion of fencing actions based upon the measurement of the fencer's own body.

What is the significance of Agrippa's combination of the authority of Euclid and Aristotle, his unwavering faith in his own intellect, and hermetic symbolism? Just as the author of an early modern fencing treatise, the hermeticist is writing for a specific audience — an "imagined community" of the sort of new man that Agrippa himself represents — one who exists outside traditional structures of academe and power. "Hermetic" symbols are used to define a community[154] — an intelligentsia, the intellectual side of Castiglione's formulation of the ideal courtier. In this case the community is textual — a vernacular "imagined community" — with a very specific political outlook. Our choices in cultural consumption, as Pierre Bourdieu writes in *La Distinction*, are a form of communication and of identification with a group. Much like modern art, Agrippa's hieroglyphics would only have been decodable to initiates.[155] He then proceeded to utilize these

---

154. Miri Rubin has noted similar tendencies for the symbol of the Eucharist in late medieval England in her *Corpus Christi: The Eucharist in Late Medieval Culture* (Cambridge: Cambridge University Press, 1991).

155. This idea of the importance of experience and observation is in harmony with the views of Nicholas Watson and others on the relationship between magic (or, as we should perhaps call it, "applied theology") and experimental science. See his "John the Monk's *Book of Visions of the Blessed and Undefiled Virgin Mary, Mother of God*," in *Conjuring Spirits: Texts and*

principles to produce a new cosmological scheme. That Agrippa didn't advance the cause of astronomy as far as he did that of fencing is of no great importance. The dialogue is only there to show us that he belongs to the same milieu as educated courtiers who believed that humanity is the mirror of creation. The services of those who had a taste for this intellectual fashion — that is, observation from nature and argument from first principles — would in time become amenable and useful to rulers such as Elizabeth I and Rudolf II, who would do much to promulagte this mode of thinking. Likewise it was opposed by those, such as Phillip II, who found legitimacy to be synonymous with orthodoxy and the landed elite and who preferred to develop a late-Scholastic worldview. Thinkers of the new breed, such as Agrippa, used ideas of numbers and geometry and argument from first principles to simultaneously re-order disciplines (such as fencing) that were of vital concern to the ruling elite and deprivilege the older structure of power-knowledge.

The implications for the Enlightenment are the same as for fencing knowledge. Agrippa personifies "Man the operator, man who seeks to draw power from the divine and natural order."[156] Aided by mathematical and geometrical demonstrations of a sort not envisioned even by Marozzo's academic lineage, and thus showing his faith in number at the core of reality, Agrippa proceeds with his "reasoning" on the art of arms in a way that takes us from first principles to the broadest possible application. And, much as for the later devotees of Newton, his disciples are those who have good reason to throw over tradition for reason. So too are their patrons, those who use their taste for such things as a marker of social status.

The *Trattato di Scientia d'Arme* of Camillo Agrippa is thus a prime example of the early modern mindset using study to control the world. Order is imposed; the trained body, governed by

---

Traditions of Medieval Magic, ed. by Claire Fanger (University Park, PA: Pennsylvania State University Press, 1998).
156. Francis A. Yates, *Girodano Bruno and the Hermetic Tradition* (Chicago: University of Chicago Press, 1964), 144.

the ruthless logic of geometry, cannot but vanquish. By art and reason, human beings control themselves and their environment, both social and physical. Agrippa did not necessarily discover new principles, but did *explain* them coherently and fashioned a pedagogy that, while appealing to the intellectual fashions of his day, would also stand the test of time. Agrippa's work is thus not only emblematic of the emerging mindset of modernity but also a lasting, beautiful, and ingenious work in its own right, for he has therein achieved the Renaissance ideal: to unify science and art to achieve understanding of, harmony with, and dominion over one's universe.

TRANSLATION NOTES

Rendering Agrippa's sixteenth-century Italian into modern English has been a difficult task. Like his contemporaries, Agrippa considered subordinated clauses and excessive verbiage to be the height of eloquence. While it did serve its purpose in the sixteenth century (and is certainly sufficiently clear to one with sufficient background), this style tends to impair the modern reader's comprehension and test his or her patience. In many instances, I found that the idea Agrippa wished to get across could be better expressed by a brief idiomatic English expression. In other places, one sentence could safely become several shorter sentences. However, in many other cases (especially in describing sequences of actions), it was necessary to retain something of the flavor of the original, even at the expense of elegant English. I ask that the reader please bear with me in such circumstances and pick his or her way carefully through these places in the text as, no doubt, Agrippa intended.

Likewise, for some purposes, a commonly understood term used in contemporary fencing could safely be substituted for a more convoluted explanation. For instance, "disengage" (or as is sometimes said, "deceive the attempt to engage") is much wieldier than "rotate it underneath the opposing sword's guard" for translating Agrippa's *girandola di sotto il fornimento de la spada contraria*. Similarly, one will notice that I have Agrippa telling us to perform our actions "*in* the time" an adversary moves (as this fencing expression preserves Agrippa's Aristotelian idea of time), instead of the more idiomatic "*at* the same time." In other cases, where a lengthy explanation is warranted or where utilizing the technical vocabulary of a different era would have distorted meaning, I have left Agrippa's explanations intact. Where Agrippa uses the same word for different meanings, the term has been translated contextually (*schifare*, for instance, can be to disengage in time, evade an attempted engagement of the blade) or to move one's body out of danger, while *professione* may be "profession" when referring to professional fencing masters, or "pursuit" when referring to fencing in general. Some technical words used by Agrippa, such as *vita*, have no modern equivalent, and have been left in the original as terms of art. Similarly, *forza* has been contextually translated as "opposition" where necessary to preserve clarity. Other terms, namely *imbrocatta* (a thrust over the arm), *mandritto* (a forehand cut), *riverso* (a backhand cut), and *stramazzone* (a straight-down cut) are commonly understood early modern fencing terms that, as they are single words that stand for many, have been left in the original. (All such terms also appear in the glossary.) Where significant deviations or idiomatic expressions need to be explained, I have made the necessary discursions in footnotes; other footnotes gloss the text, give the original technical terms, and explain Agrippa's intellectual background. In all cases, however, emphasis has been on preserving meaning and technical precision.

One of the largest changes has been from the impersonal third-person *questo* ("one" or "our fencer") in Part I to the more contemporary English second-person "you." This makes the text both less confusing and more appealing to the modern reader, though it can unfortunately give the appearance of a teach-yourself book — which Agrippa's work most definitely is not, being more of a technical work written for those who already had knowledge both of humanistic studies and of arms. The second part of the treatise can also be somewhat confusing since Agrippa refers to both the various postures by letter and the fencers by the letter of their initial position, and so I have clarified by specifying (for instance) the "position of G" or "the fencer who was in A."

For those wishing to peruse the original text, it is downloadable from the Raymond J. Lord collection hosted by the University of Massachussetts Amherst Center for Renaissance Studies, at http://www.umass.edu/renaissance/lord/collection.html. I shall also maintain a page of errata, amendations, and discussion on my own website, historicalfencing.org.

BIBLIOGRAPHY

Manuscripts

Letter of Girolamo Muzio to Cosimi I de' Medici, Archivio di Stato di Firenze, Mediceo del Principato 401, f. 151.

Florius de arte lutandi, Bibliothèque National de France MS Lat. 11269.

Hanko Döbringers Fechtbuch vom 1389, Germanisches Nationalmuseum Nürnberger Handschrift Cod. HS 3227a.

Hans Talhoffers Alte Armatur und Ringkunst, MS Thott 290 2, Kongelige Bibliotek, Copenhagen.

Jud Lews Fechtbuch, Universitätsbibliothek Augsburg Cod. I.6.4.3.

Primary Sources

Agocchie, Giovanni dall'. *Dell'arte di scrimia*. Venice, 1572.

Agrippa, Camillo. *Trattato di scienza d'arme*. Rome, 1553.

—. *Trattato di transportar la guglia*. Rome, 1583.

Alberti, Leon Baptisa. *Leonis Baptistæ Alberti opera inedita*. Edited by Girolamo Mancini. Florence: J.C. Sansoni, 1890.

Altoni, Francesco di Sandro. *Monomachia:Trattato dell'arte di scherma*. Edited by Alessandro Battistini, Massimo Rubboli, and Iacopo Venni. Rimini: Il Cerchio, 2007.

Anonimo Bolognese. *L'arte della spada*. Edited by Marco Rubboli and Luca Cesari. Rimini: Il Cerchio, 2005.

Bolzani, Giovanni Piero Valeriano. *Hieroglyphica*. Basel, 1556.

Calvacabo, Hieronimo. *Traité ou instruction pour tirer des armes*. Rouen, 1597, 1617.

Capo Ferro, Ridolfo. *Italian Rapier Combat*. Translated by Jared Kirby. London: Greenhill Books, 2004. (Translation of Capo Ferro's *Gran Simulacro*, 1610.)

Caro, Annibale. *Lettere Familiares*. Edited by Aulo Greco. 3 vols. Florence: Le Monnier, 1959–61.

Caroso, Fabrito. *Il ballarino* (Venice, 1581). Online facsimile and transcription by Greg Lindhal. http://www.pbm.com/~lindahl/caroso/ (accessed July 17, 2007).

——. *La Nobiltà di Dame* (Venice, 1600). Online facsimile and transcription by Greg Lindhal. http://www.pbm.com/~lindahl/caroso2/ (accessed July 17, 2007).

Carranza, Jéronimo de. *De la filosophia de las armas*. Seville, 1582.

Castglione, Baldesare. *Libro del cortegiano*. Edited by Giulio Carnazzi. Milan: Biblioteca Universale Rizzoli, 1987.

Cesariano, Cesare. *Di Lucío Vítruvío Pollíone de archítectura libri dece traductí de latíno in vulgare affigurati*. Como, 1521.

Colonna, Francesco. *Hypnerotomachia Poliphili*. Venice, 1499. http://mitpress.mit.edu/e-books/HP/index.htm (accessed Apr. 10, 2007).

Fabris, Salvatore. *The Art of Dueling*. Translated by Tomasso Leoni. Highland Park, TX: Chivalry Bookshelf, 2005. (Translation of Fabris' *Lo Schermo*, 1606.)

Fiore di Liberi. *Flos duellatorium*. Pierpont-Morgan MS M.383. Transcription available at: http://www.the-exiles.org/FioreProject/Project.htm (accessed Apr. 7, 2007).

Florio, John. *New World of Words*. London, 1611.

G.A. *Pallas armata*. London, 1639.

Forgeng Jeffrey L. *The Medieval Art of Swordsmanship: A Facsimile and Translation of Royal Armouries MS I.33*. Union City, CA: Chivalry Bookshelf, 2003.

Froissart, Jean. *Oeuvres*. Edited by Kervyn de Lettenhove. 25 vols. Brussels, 1867–77.

Grassi, Giacomo di. *Ragione di adoprar sicuramente l'arme, si da offesa come da difesa*. Venice, 1570.

Horapollo, and Pietro Vasolli. *Oro Apolline Niliaco delli segni Hierogliphici, cioe delle significationi di scolture sacre appresso gli Egittij*. Venice: Gabriel de Ferrari, 1547. http://www.studiolum.com/en/cd08-horapollo.htm (accessed Apr. 10, 2007).

Joly, Barthélemy. *Voyage en Espagne*. Revue Hispanique 20 (1909): 460–618.

Lespinasse, René. *Les Métiers et corporations de la ville de Paris*. 3 vols. Paris: Imprimerie Nationale, 1897.

Manciolino, Antonio. *Opera nova*. Bologna, 1531.

Marozzo, Achille. *Opera nova*. Modena, 1536.

Meyer, Joachim. *The Art of Combat: A German Martial Arts Treatise of 1570*. Translated by Jeffrey Forgeng New York: Palgrave Macmillan, 2006. (Translation of Meyer's *Gründtliche Beschreibung*. Strasbourg, 1570.)

Monte, Pietro. *Exercitiorum atque artis militaris collectanea*. Milan, 1509.

Muzio, Girolamo. *Il duello*. Venice, 1550.

Negri, Cesare. *Le gratie d'amore/Nuove inventioni di balli*. Venice, 1602/1604. Facsimile, concordance and transcription by Greg Lindhal. http://www.pbm.com/~lindahl/negri/ (accessed July 17, 2007).

Novati, Francesco. *Flos duellatorum*. Bergamo: Istituto Italiano d'Arti Grafiche, 1902. (Facsimile of Fiore dei Liberi's *Flos Duellatorum*, c. 1410.)

Pacheco de Narváez, Luis. *Carta al duque de cea diciendo su parecer acerca del libro de Geronimo de Carrança*. Madrid, 1618.

—. *Nueva ciencia y filosofia de la destreza de las armas*. Madrid, 1672.

Pérez Pastor, Cristóbal. *Bibliografía madrileña ó descripción de las obras impresas en Madrid* 3 (1621–25). Reprinted in *Revista de archivos, bibliotecas y museos* (1907): 251.

Picinelli, Filippo. *Ateneo dei letterati Milanesi*. Milan, 1670.

Pigna, Giovan Battista. *Il duello*. Venice, 1554.

Saviolo, Vincent. *His Practice*. London, 1595.

Silver, George. *Paradoxes of Defence*. London, 1599.

Thibault, Girard. *Academy of the Sword*. Translated by John Michael Greer. Highland Park, TX: Chivalry Bookshelf, 2007. (Translation of Thibault's *La académie de la espée*, 1628.)

Titi, Filippo. *Descrizione delle pitture, sculture e architetture esposte in Roma*. Rome; Marco Pagliarini, 1674. Edited by Bill Thayer. http://penelope.uchicago.edu/Thayer/I/Gazetteer/Places/Europe/Italy/Lazio/Roma/Rome/_Texts/Titi/1763*/home.html (accessed July 17, 2007).

Tudor Royal Proclamations. Edited by Hughes, Paul L and James F. Larkin. New Haven: Yale University Press, 1969.

Vadi, Filipo. *Arte gladiatoria dimicandi*. Translated by Greg Mele and Luca Porzo. Highland Park, TX: Chivalry Bookshelf, 2002. (Translation and facsimile of Vadi's *Arte Gladiatoria Dimicandi*, c. 1482–1487.)

Vegetius Renatus, Publius Flavius. *Epitoma rei militaris*. Edited by C. Lang. Stuttgart: Teubner, 1885. Edited by Mike Bishop. http://armatura.connectfree.co.uk/protoveg/ (accessed July 17, 2007).

Viggiani, Angelo. *Lo schermo.* Venice, 1575.

Vitruvius, Marcus Polio. *De Architectura.* Edited by Valentin Rose. Leipzig: Teubner, 1899.

—. *De Architectura.* Edited by Bill Thayer. http://penelope.uchicago.edu/Thayer/L/Roman/Texts/Vitruvius/ (accessed July 17, 2007).

SECONDARY WORKS

Amberger, J. Christopher. *The Secret History of the Sword.* Baltimore: Hammerterz Verlag, 1997.

Angelozzi, Giancarlo, and Cesarina Casanova. *La nobiltà disciplinata.* Bologna: CLUEB, 2003.

Anglo, Sydney. "The Man Who Taught Leonardo Darts: Pietro Monti and His 'Lost' Fencing Book." *The Antiquaries Journal* 59.2 (1989): 261–78.

—. *The Martial Arts of Renaissance Europe.* New Haven: Yale University Press, 2000.

Ashby, Thomas. "The Bodelian MS. of Pirro Ligorio." *The Journal of Roman Studies* 9 (1919): 181–82.

Billacois, François. *Le duel dans la société française des XVIe-XVIIe siècles. Essai de psychosociologie historique.* Paris: École des Hautes Études en Sciences Sociales, 1986.

Brand Paul. "The Jewish Community in the Records of English Royal Government." *The Jews in Medieval Britain: Historical, Literary and Archaeological Perspectives.* Ed. by Patricia Skinner. Rochester, NY: Boydell & Brewer, 2003.

Briost, Pascal, Hervé Drévillon, and Pierre Serna. *Croiser le fer: Violence et culture de l'épée dans la France moderne (XVIe–XVIIIe siècle).* Seyssel: Champ Vallon, 2002.

Brown, Donald E. *Human Universals.* New York: McGraw-Hill, 1991.

Brunet, Jacques-Charles. *Manuel du librarie et de l'amateur de livres.* 7 vols. Paris: Librarie de Firmin Didot Frères, 1860–1878.

Bryson, Frederick R. *The Sixteenth-Century Italian Duel.* Chicago: University of Chicago Press, 1938.

Capek, Milic. "The Conflict between the Absolutist and the Relational Theory of Time before Newton." *Journal of the History of Ideas* 48:4 (Oct. 1987): 595–608.

Carruthers, Mary J. *The Book of Memory.* Cambridge: Cambridge University Press, 1990.

Castle, Egerton. *Schools and Masters of Fence*. London: G. Bell and Sons, 1885; reprint as *Schools and Masters of Fencing*, Mineola, NY: Dover Publications, 2003.

Cavina, Marco. *Il duello giudiziario per punto d'onore*. Turin: G. Giappichelli, 2003.

Celenza, Christopher. "Pythagoras in the Renaissance: The Case of Marsilio Ficino." *Renaissance Quarterly* 52:3 (Autumn 1999): 667–711.

Cirillo, Giuseppe. "Postille a Carlo Urbino e osservazioni sulla pittura cremesca del '500 in relazione con Genova." *Parma per l'arte* 13.1 (2007): 25–46.

Curtis, Mary Dill, and R.E. "Puck" Curtis. *Destreza Translation and Research Project*. San Jose, CA: Ghost Sparrow Publications. http://www.destreza. us (accessed Mar. 18, 2008).

Dales, Richard C. "Time and Eternity in the Thirteenth Century." *Journal of the History of Ideas* 49.1 (Jan.-Mar. 1988): 27–45.

Dekker, Dirk-Jan. "Buridan's Concept of Time. Time, Motion and the Soul in John Buridan's Questions on Aristotle's *Physics*" in *The Metaphysics and Natural Philosophy of John Buridan*. Ed. by Johannes M.M.H. Thijssen and Jack Zupko. Leiden: Brill, 2001, 151–63.

Deforneaux, Marcelin. *Daily Life in Spain in the Golden Age*. Translated by Newton Branch. Stanford: Stanford University Press, 1979.

Donati, Claudio. *L'idea di nobiltà in Italia*. Rome: Laterza, 1988.

Draeger, Donn F. *Classical Bujutsu*. New York: Weatherhill, 1973.

—. *Comprehensive Asian Fighting Arts*. New York: Kodansha International, 1980.

—, and Robert W. Smith. *Asian Fighting Arts*. Tokyo: Kodansha International, 1969.

Fragnito, Gigliola. "Cardinals' Courts in Sixteenth-Century Rome." *The Journal of Modern History* 65 (Mar. 1993): 26–56.

Gay, Peter. *The Enlightenment: An Interpretation*. 2 vols. New York: Random House, 1966-69; revised ed. New York: Norton, 1995.

Geertz, Clifford. "Deep Play: Notes on the Balinese Cockfight." In *The Interpretation of Cultures*. New York: Basic Books, 1973, 412–53.

Gelli, Jacopo. "Un trattato di scherma con postille autografe di Torquato Tasso." *La lettura* 1 (1901): 1113-20.

Gingerich, Owen. *The Book Nobody Read*. New York: Walker & Company, 2004.

Grossman, Dave. *On Killing: The Psychological Cost of Learning to Kill in War and Society.* Boston: Little, Brown, 1996.

Hairston, Julia L. "Out of the Archive: Four Newly-Identified Figures in Tullia d'Aragona's *Rime della Signora Tullia di Aragona et di diversi a lei* (1547)." *MLN* 118.1 (Jan. 2003): 257–63.

Hanlon, Gregory. "The Decline of a Provincial Military Aristocracy: Siena 1560–1740." *Past and Present* 155 (May 1997): 64–108.

Heninger, S. K., Jr. "Some Renaissance Versions of the Pythagorean Tetrad." *Studies in the Renaissance* 8 (1961): 7–35.

Hodges, Kenneth. "Chivalric Convection: Sir Philip Sidney's Response to Popular Fencing." Paper presented at the International Congress on Medieval Studies, Kalamazoo, MI, 2006.

Holmer, Joan Ozark. "'Draw if ye be Men': Saviolo's Significance for *Romeo and Juliet.*" *Shakespeare Quarterly* 45. 2 (Summer 1994): 163–89.

Huizinga, Johan. *Homo Ludens.* Boston: Beacon Press, 1962.

Jacks, Philip J. "The *Simulacrum* of Fabio Calvo: A View of Roman Architecture all'antica in 1527." *The Art Bulletin* 72.3. (Sept. 1990): 453–81.

Keen, Maurice. *Chivalry.* New Haven: Yale University Press, 1984.

La Rocca, Donald J. *The Academy of the Sword: Illustrated Fencing Books 1500–1800.* New York: Metropolitan Museum of Art, 1998.

Leoni, Tommaso. "Notes on the Judicial Duel in Italy." Paper presented at the International Swordfighting and Martial Arts Convention, Lansing, MI, Aug. 3–6, 2006. http://www.salvatorfabris.com/forum/viewtopic. php?t=104url (accessed Mar. 18, 2007.)

Levi, Giorgio Enrico, and Jacopo Gelli. *Bibliografia del duello.* Milan: Ulrico Hoepli, 1903.

Lochner, Karl E. *Die Entwicklungsphasen der europäischen Fechtkunst.* Vienna: Selbstverlag des Verfassers, 1953.

Lombardi, Leonardo. "Camillo Agrippa's Hydraulic Inventions on the Pincian Hill (1574–1578)." Trans. by Katherine W. Rinne. *The Waters of Rome* 5 (Apr. 2008). http://www.iath.virginia.edu/rome/ Journal5LombardiNew.pdf (accessed June 8, 2009).

Martînez, Ramón. "Jeronimo de Carranza's 'Philosophy' of Arms." http://www.martinez-destreza.com/articles/carranza.htm (accessed Mar. 18, 2007).

Michaux, Marie-Anne. "Private Armouries: Arms and Armour in the Parisian Domestic Interior (1515–1547)." M.A. thesis, Royal College of Art, 2005.

Morison, Stanley. *Four Centuries of Fine Printing.* 4th ed. New York: Barnes and Noble, 1960.

Mortimer, Ruth. *Catalogue of Books and Manuscripts.* 2 Vol. Cambridge, MA: Harvard University Press, 1964.

Muhlberger, Steven. *Deeds of Arms.* Highland Village, TX: Chivalry Bookshelf, 2005.

Muir, Edward. *Mad Blood Stirring.* Baltimore: Johns Hopkins University Press, 1993.

Norman, A.V.B. *The Rapier and Small-Sword, 1460–1820.* New York: Arno Press, 1980.

Oakeshott, Ewart. *The Sword in the Age of Chivalry.* London: Lutterworth Press, 1964; reprint ed.: Mineola, NY: Dover Publications, 1996.

Panofsky, Erwin. *The Codex Huygens and Leonardo da Vinci's Art Theory.* Studies of the Warburg Institute 13. London: Warburg Institute, 1940.

Pantanelli, Guido. "Scherma e maestri di scherma Bolognese." *Strenna storica Bolognese* 3 (1930): 45–49.

Patridge, Loren. "Divinity and Dynasty at Caprarola: Perfect History in the Room of Farnese Deeds." *The Art Bulletin* 60.3 (Sept. 1978): 494–530.

—. "The Room of Maps at Caprarola, 1573–75." *The Art Bulletin* 77.3 (Sept. 1995): 413–44.

—. "The Farnese Circular Courtyard in Caprarola: God, Geopolitics, Genealogy, and Gender." *The Art Bulletin* 83.2 (Jan. 2001): 259–93.

Phillips, John Goldsmith, and Olga Raggio. "Ottavio Farnese." *The Metropolitan Museum of Art Bulletin,* New Series 12.8. (Apr. 1954): 233–40.

Quinlan-McGrath, Mary. "Caprarola's Salla della Cosmografia." *Renaissance Quarterly* 50.4 (Winter 1997): 1-45–1100.

Ragghianti, C. L. "Scherma con geometria." *Critica d'arte* 147–49 (1976): 88–92.

Richards, Jennifer. "Assumed Simplicity and the Critique of Nobility: Or, How Castiglione Read Cicero." *Renaissance Quarterly* 54.2 (Summer 2001): 460–86.

Rogers, Clifford J., ed. *The Military Revolution Debate: Readings on the Military Transformation of Early Modern Europe.* Boulder, CO: Westview Press, 1995.

Rubin, Miri. *Corpus Christi: The Eucharist in Late Medieval Culture.* Cambridge: Cambridge University Press, 1991.

Rubin, Patricia. "The Private Chapel of Cardinal Alessandro Farnese in the Cancelleria, Rome." *Journal of the Warburg and Courtauld Institutes* 50 (1987): 82–112.

Smail, Daniel Lord. "Factions and Vengeance in Renaissance Italy: A Review Article." *Comparative Studies in Society and History* 38.4 (Oct. 1996): 781–89.

——. *The Consumption of Justice: Emotions, Publicity, and Legal Culture in Marseille, 1264–1423.* Ithaca: Cornell University Press, 2003.

——. "Scuole di scherma in Milano nel 1474." *Bollettino storico della Svizzera Italiana* 7 (1885): 118.

Steckel, Richard H. "New Light on the 'Dark Ages': The Remarkably Tall Stature of Northern European Men during the Medieval Era." *Social Science History* 28.2 (Summer 2004): 211–28.

Stinger, Charles. *The Renaissance in Rome.* Bloomington: Indianan University Press, 1985.

Summers, David. "*Contrapposto:* Style and Meaning in Renaissance Art." *The Art Bulletin* 59.3 (Sept. 1977): 336-61.

Thimm, Carl A. *A Complete Bibliography of Fencing and Dueling.* London: John Lane, 1896.

Tietze-Conrat, Erica. "Neglected Contemporary Sources Relating to Michelangelo and Titian." *The Art Bulletin* 25.2 (June 1943): 156–59.

Warner, Gordon, and Donn F. Draeger. *Japanese Swordsmanship.* New York: Weatherhill, 1982.

Watson, Nicholas. "John the Monk's *Book of Visions of the Blessed and Undefiled Virgin Mary, Mother of God.*" In *Conjuring Spirits: Texts and Traditions of Medieval Magic.* Edited by Claire Fanger. University Park, PA: The Pennsylvania State University Press, 1998.

Yates, Francis A. *Giordano Bruno and the Hermetic Tradition.* Chicago: University of Chicago Press, 1964.

FENCING

A RENAISSANCE TREATISE

MOTU PROPIO OF
PHILLIP SALUTIARUM

TEN-YEAR PROHIBITION AGAINST
PRINTING AND SELLING

It has come to our attention that our dear son Camillo Agrippa of Milan has composed this work, on the Science of Arms, which explains the science and art of arms and other exercises with mathematical demonstrations and many other explanations and diagrams, and that he intends to publish it shortly. Nothing like this work has ever been seen either in modern or in ancient times, and he has produced it by many long nights of hard work and by the greatest ability and effort. Therefore, on account of the aforesaid, in order that Camillo might be motivated to undertake other works and that he justly obtain some profit from this one, and wishing to reward and honor him with a special privilege, we concede to him that any faithful publisher and press he might choose to print this work shall be the only publisher and printer with the ability to print and license to sell it. We also forbid all other publishers, booksellers, and other persons save for Camillo and his chosen press — no matter what their status, rank, order, or situation — to dare to print this work in order to offer it for sale. The penalty shall be excommunication both in our lands and everywhere else, loss of the books, and a fine of forty ducats of gold *de camera* for printers and fifty for booksellers for each violation, payable to Camillo and his aforesaid chosen press.[1] We forbid the latter from either charging anyone with this order or applying the penalties without another declaration from us. Rather, we order the governors, senators, and tribunes in charge of the welfare of the City to aid Camillo and his chosen publisher if they should require

---

1. Literally, gold ducats "of the chamber," that is, from the official papal mint and governed by the papal court. Fifty gold ducats was a large sum for an ordinary man.

anything else for executing the abovesaid penalties, and to take care to enforce this *motu propio* inviolably unless it is contradicted by other decrees and apostolic orders.

If it please Jesus.

Ph[illip] Salutiarum[2]

---

2. "Salutiarum" means "of Saluzzo," identifying the signatory as most likely Filippo Archinto, bishop of Saluzzo and vicar-general of Rome.

DEDICATION LETTER OF CAMILLO AGRIPPA

To the Most Illustrious and Excellent
Lord Cosimo de Medici, Duke of Florence

O my most illustrious and excellent lord, who, it seems to me,
has no equal:

Because[3] of the diabolical modern invention of artillery, all
that remains to us of the good ancient ways of military honor is
the duel — and that corrupted and spoiled by the calumny of
cartelli. Therefore, I have busied myself in remedying the situation
however I can. Using whatever small ability that nature, or God,
has granted me, I have shown how a man can defend himself with
skill, with art, and with valor either in a formal trial by combat[4] or
in an unforeseen armed assault. Thus, one can defeat the enemy so
that he will be forced to ask for quarter as if he has been thrown to
the ground and beaten. Because the world knows that your most
worthy ancestors were true restorers of good letters, good scientific
studies, and valuable languages, and that you, accompanying arms
with letters, are the true sustainer of both, it seems proper to me
to dedicate my work to your excellency's most renowned name.
God grant all your honest desire.

In Rome,
March 15, 1553
Your excellency the duke's most humble servant,
Camillo Agrippa

---

3. The first word of this paragraph in the original edition is "Poi," and
its capital "P" has an image of Aeneas carrying his father from the burning
of Troy — the very image of filial piety.

4. *Ne gli steccati*, literally, "in the *steccati*," that is, a palisade or closed field
(cognate with the English *stocade*) within which a formal, legally ordained
trial by combat would take place. The use of such arenas, seen in many
medieval and early modern fencing treatises, served to create a space where
violence could be literally corralled, separated from society at large.

Fig. 4. Agrippa Disputing against the Philosophers.

PREFACE

The science of arms consists principally of justice, secondly of knowledge, and thirdly of practice. Since each man ought to be just in his own conduct, it is not my present intention to discuss justice. We therefore proceed to the use of arms. This is called the auxiliary remedy, to be used when all others are found wanting and the matter is worthy of such treatment, or when it is necessary for self-defense — as the law (under which I place myself) states clearly. However, I say with utmost certainty that although reason, experience (that small help), art and genius might be accompanied by a valiant spirit, they are not always found together with justice. Thus, the case of the miserable cavaliers who feuded solely out of pride or — as we say — arrogance, with the result being the opposite of what they had wished. In place of honor, they acquired manifest infamy.

But since discussing this is not my objective, I come to the second part, which concerns the knowledge of arms. This knowledge is the life and the victory of he who uses it, and is all contained in this, my work. However, it does not seem necessary to me to discuss this in an overly long prologue, since from part to part, following the logical order of the work, it will be made obvious in the third part. This consists of practical application and is very different from the writings from which it is derived. For this reason, it is necessary for everyone who wishes for honor in whichever science and art, after being well apprised of the theory, makes it come alive with practice. Therefore let each skillful pilgrim pay close attention to my new discovery, presented here in two separate parts. I pray to God, with Justice interceding,[5] that it will be both useful and delightful, as I have intended.

---

5. That is, the personification of justice intervening in the manner of a saint.

BOOK 1

CHAPTER 1

CONCERNING THE FOUR PRINCIPAL GUARDS

To begin, I propose four primary guards to be used in this exercise: first, second, third, and fourth. These are shown in the following figure, each marked by a letter — the first by A, the second by B, the third by C, and the fourth by D. For the rest of the work, these letters will stand in place of saying first, second, third, and fourth guard. The reason why they are so-named is because anyone who in anger draws the sword he wears at his side, whether because of his own fury or some external provocation of word or deed, will raise his hand to form a guard. Because this is the first that can be made after clearing the sword from the scabbard, it is called "first." Lowering the hand a little so that the arm is at the same height as the shoulder is the second. By slightly lowering the sword-hand and moving it to the outside and closer to the knee, you will make the third. Finally, moving the sword-hand inside the knee makes the fourth. These are the primary guards because many others can be made from them, depending to the situation.[6]

Similarly, in discussing the general, offensive and defensive actions derived from each of these, we can simply mention the letter corresponding to the figure as they are here, such as "D" denoting the last of the four primaries. Thus, we will not need to repeat the plates for every figure, guard, action, or movement of the body that one ought to practice in order to defend oneself and harm the enemy — that is, moving from first to second, from second to third, from third to fourth, or conversely, from first to third or fourth, or from second to fourth or first. Also, in some circumstances it may be more advantageous to use another movement derived from the aforesaid primaries, modifying them as will be described later.

---

6.   The rotation of the hand (though not the position or elevation) correspond to the hand positions of *prima, seconda, terza*, and *quarta*. This later becomes standard in all Italian fencing.

Fig. 5. The Four Guards.

Although some of these actions may seem difficult to perform, nonetheless you should take care to practice them well, as all aid a man who heeds the points, lines, times, and measure that ultimately govern this activity. The proof of this statement will be seen in the double figures that follow after the simple figures in the second book of the treatise. In these double figures, the letters are placed at the heads or the feet of the figures so you can understand how the primary guards are used, as well as how to perform the various techniques that are derived from them (while always taking care to heed the aforesaid points, lines, times, and so on). So, although more A's, more B's, more C's, and other duplicate letters are seen with the simple figures, these do not indicate new guards or actions or movements of the body different from the primaries or the actions derived from them. One can easily make the mistake of thinking that these figures show new sorts of guards, since they show two enemies fighting with one figure positioned in one sort of guard or attack in one part of the closed field (or in whatever

9

other place they might be fighting), and the other, on the other side, performing another attack or guard. However, they are one and the same figure, defined only once. If you remember the actions previously denoted by the letters, you can very easily correct any false impression. They are shown according to their position in space in the same way that anything shows a new perspective when it is seen from a little in front or to the rear or to the side because of some movement or action that it might make (except for a ball, which, though turned to any side, shows nothing other than light or dark).

Chapter 2

Concerning a Geometrical Figure

As I stated previously, this pursuit is ultimately governed by points, lines, times, measures, and so forth, and comes from thinking in a mathematical — which is to say, a geometrical — fashion. Therefore, before we proceed any further, I will explain how points, lines, and so on affect this art so that what I say below might be more easily understood. In order to better demonstrate this and to show how you can make a better (which is to say, a longer) attack, I have prepared the following half-figure [Fig. 6].

The lines marked with the letters that extend forward horizontally from the figure's arm represent the sword held in the hand with the arm extended. As seen in the figure, you can move the point forward, forming a straight line, and then move it further by means of the angle formed by the bend between the torso and the thigh. The two lines that form this angle are the one that runs from the point of the sword and the one that runs from the sole of the foot along the leg. The angle is formed by moving the leg either a half-step[7] or a full ordinary step or a forced step.[8] As I have already

---

7.   A *mezzo passo*, which is, as Agrippa explains later, half an ordinary step.
8.   The "forced" step, elsewhere described as a "firm" (*ferma*) attack, is the long step previously described, thus lengthening and providing impetus to the attack.

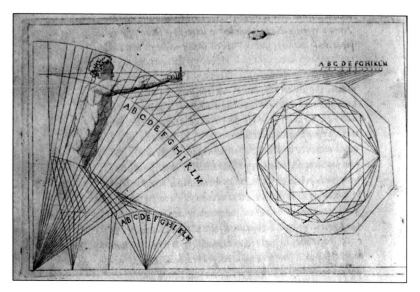

Fig. 6. A Geometrical Figure.

said, this can be seen by the lines in the half-figure by following each from A to A, from B to B, and so on. Since the length of the line always remains the same between identical letters, the point moves forward by the same amount as you move your body forward with a half-step. Also, the point will move forward in proportion to how acute the angle becomes. In other words, you will move forward against the enemy by the same amount as you push the step forward,[9] and the amount you lower your body. How the ordinary step, the half-step, and the extraordinary step are used will be demonstrated in the course of explaining the various actions.

As seen in the figure, the two lines formed by the sword and

---

9.   In this case, I have elected to translate *spingere* ("push") literally due to the fact that he is talking about moving forward on the step. Agrippa uses this term *spingere* throughout to indicate a thrust, though we have chosen to translate it more idiomatically as the sort of attack that is intended. Elsewhere, *spingere* is rendered contextually as "thrust."

the feet form an acute angle. It's not that I don't see that there is an obtuse angle and two acute, rather I have explained it this way so you can see what happens if you lower yourself more or less. The additional advantage gained by lengthening the step and leaning forwards is shown with a duplicate letter. The other point shows the end of the extra reach, and those below it indicate how much further forward you can thrust by extending the step forward. You can therefore see the distance an ordinary half-step goes forward between the first and second points. However, the lines that go out from the middle of the figure's torso form a pyramid and show the effect of moving the leg, not a many-legged monster. Therefore, let me explain that the space between the second point and the third is equal to another half, and that both of these half-steps make an ordinary step. The space between the third and the last point (not moving the first point) measures a third of a forced step, which is equal to half an ordinary step (that is, from the first point to the second). Thus, three ordinary half-steps make an extraordinary step, and a third of an extraordinary step is half of an ordinary.

CHAPTER 3

CONCERNING ANOTHER GEOMETRICAL FIGURE

The following figure [Fig. 7] specifically shows what was not so easily seen in the previous one: that bending the knee, rather than holding it straight, increases the line forward slightly. The more you bend it (while also extending your arm), the more the line moves towards the enemy. As above, the point of the sword moves forward in proportion to how far the knee bends, with the distance always remaining the same between one letter and another—that is, from B to B, from C to C, and so on.

What happens if we move the arm the opposite way? By straightening the leg, as shown in the diagram, and by retracting the arm, as shown by the letters, little by little the line becomes shortened. The greater the angle between the hand and the arm,

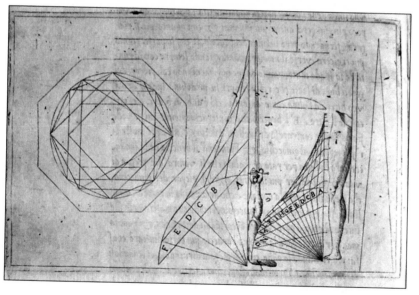

Fig. 7. Another Geometrical Figure.

horter the line. The same happens if we withdraw the leg —
is, straighten the knee and not lean forward at the waist.

A warning to those who think it is correct to extend their
sword-arms with their wrists slightly bent[10]: You cannot bend your
hand or arm in any way without raising your sword at least a quarter
or half a *palma* away from the enemy's. One should therefore train
oneself to extend the hand as far as possible and keep the arm as
straight as possible. If you do otherwise you help your adversary,
to your own harm and great peril.

CHAPTER 4

CONCERNING THE FIRST GUARD DENOTED BY A

In a previous figure [Fig. 5], I explained the four primary guards,
marking each with a letter of the alphabet. I also explained the
reasons for their names and their order, why they are the primary
guards and how the other guards are derived from them, and
promised that I would show the principles of this work with single
figures and the application in double figures. I also showed how
to shorten and lengthen the line of attack, using the geometrical
figures as examples. We therefore proceed to how to use the first
guard, shown below in its own figure [Fig.8], in self-defense.

You might be curious about the little fork of wood drawn
next to the figure of the first guard, since I have not explained its
presence and it seems to be rather extraneous to our discussion.
Therefore, let me explain that it is there to encourage by word and
example those people who think themselves unfit to study arms
because of their nature or some other inherent indisposition. The
stick is placed alongside the four guards because a piece of wood,
taken unfinished from a tree and not having had any work done to
it, provided that it is straight and strong enough to be used with a
light hand, is quite sufficient to make all sorts of geometrical figures
such as circles, squares, triangles, octagons (from which you can

---

10. With the wrist "broken," as is sometimes said.

Fig. 8. The First Guard (A).

similarly make a proportional sphere), and so on. Similarly, anyone who has their eyes open will see that I am right when I say that a man, governing himself with reason and art, ought to perform this activity well.[11]

I would have told you how to make this figure,[12] but feared that it might seem that I want to discuss geometry rather than arms, and that you might think we will spend all day discussing all sorts of subjects. Free yourself from this misconception! I am only using this example to encourage everybody not to excuse themselves on account of some bodily inability or natural deficiency (the varieties of which are too numerous to discuss) from always practicing this art as best they can — for if used for the right reason and according

11. In other words, Agrippa is saying that, like geometry, the basis of the art is so sound that even a poor instrument — an unskilled man — abiding by its precepts cannot help but perform agreeably.
12. Agrippa, in fact, gives the method in the dialogue at the end of the treatise.

to the principles of this work, it can, heaven permitting, prolong your life and, if it is in the stars, exchange life for death.

Now that we have come to the discussion of the first guard, let me respond to those who say that in order to make a thrust, you need first to go on guard in a medium stance,[13] holding your right arm behind you crooked or bent over your right shoulder. These people say that by going on guard this way and finishing the step with the right foot and the hand low to the ground — or, as certain others claim, not doing this—the *imbroccata*, or overhand thrust, succeeds more easily, more strongly, and more securely. I say, however, that by going on guard according to the figure, you make a better and more secure *imbroccata*. In fact, you so disadvantage the adversary that you need not fear any man. Also, it does not put you at any disadvantage yourself. The reason why it is better is because it extends further forward and does not turn backwards any. This is because, just as in the figure, a straight line is longer and also quicker. If you look at the illustration, you will see that, according to my reckoning, by keeping your sword-arm directed at the enemy in the first guard with your feet close together and your left hand (which will sometimes have a dagger, and sometimes, as in the figure, not hold anything[14]) in front of your chest, you will be a half- or quarter-step further from the adversary, depending on your stance. By staying in a narrow stance, you will gain as much as a *palmo* of reach against the enemy and thus be able to make a better attack.[15] Also, by staying in narrow first, you can move forward and backward as you have to with the same step more quickly and without moving your left foot back, running back, or sliding back. This first guard makes the body firmer and lets you defend yourself without having to parry the attack.

---

13. Literally, *passo*, "step." Agrippa prefers the right foot to be always in front, with the feet spaced narrowly (*stretta*) or close together when one is in first (*prima guardia*), whereas those he argues against here prefer a *mezzo passo*—literally meaning a "half-" or "medium" step, but here used as "stance."
14. Actually, the figure *is* holding a dagger.
15. Agrippa literally says *spinger contra con maggior passo* "push a better step against [him]."

Also, by keeping your hand forward, you can defend yourself with the half of the sword closest to the hilt, which is the stronger part. Both the arm and the weapon are strong enough to withstand a blow, and you can also still attack the enemy while defending yourself with them at the same time. On the other hand, no one can deny that by holding your sword behind you, you can only defend yourself with the half of the sword closest to the point, which is the weakest part and presents the most danger to you.[16]

Therefore, you should not go on guard as they say you should, for, though you can make a more powerful attack by holding your arm behind you, this violates the true principle of always threatening the adversary with the point either to hit him or keep him far away.[17] Rather, holding it behind you in order to turn and push forwards again is not a good idea, since it has two great disadvantages: it loses you time and makes it easier for the enemy to hit you while not being hit himself.

Moreover, some people say they can raise a man out of a guard in which he holds his hand extended in this way by cutting with *mandritti* and *riversi*, with defensive weapons such as the dagger or the cape, or by seizing the blade with a *guanto di presa*. I reply that this is nonsense, for, as I have often repeated, someone who tries to beat the point of your sword aside with *mandritti* is only fooling themselves. That is because you can, in a single action, without moving your arm any, lower the point a little bit to evade the enemy's sword, aim at his right side, extend your arm while rotating your hand, and step forwards with your right foot to hit him.[18] Attack

---

16.   Agrippa's discussion of the two parts of the sword roughly corresponds to the traditional division of the *forte*, or strong, which can exert greater lever action over the opposing steel, and the *debole*, or weak, the part with which one strikes but which is vulnerable to the adversary's levering.

17.   Note here also the parallels to Vegetius' explanation of how Roman soldiers were trained to thrust instead of cut.

18.   *Schifar* (avoid) *la spada contraria* — here, the *cavatione di tempo* or disengagement in time. Calvacabo later notes the widespread belief that Agrippa invented this technique, but from context it seems that Agrippa expects this to be an obvious and well-known answer to such an attack. I have translated this contextually as "disengage."

anyone who tries to beat the sword aside with a *riverso* or do any of the other actions mentioned above in the same way, by keeping your arm steady but aiming at his left side. (This does not apply to the cape or the round shield or the buckler, which cover the whole body of the man using them and so require other methods, which will be discussed in their proper place.)

Moreover, when you cannot use this technique to defend yourself, then lower the sword from the first guard into second and, receiving the *mandritto* close to the hilt, take a transverse step to the right with your right foot and hit him with a thrust to the chest. Also, if the enemy wants to seize your blade or beat your point aside with his left hand or a dagger or any of the other things I mentioned above, then in the same time that he goes to do this, take a traverse step with your right foot to your right side, and you can, while voiding your body, give him a thrust below the waist in fourth.

Some people say that by going on guard in first with your feet close together, you make it easier for the enemy to hit you in the chest by attacking on the outside of the cross with the false edge.[19] However, by using your true edge[20] to press his point to the outside, you can give him a thrust below in first. Also, some people say that by holding your hand in front, you can be wounded by a cut or thrust to the hand or arm. I say that in either case, if you step back into a wide or medium stance without joining your feet, then he must oppose[21] your blade with his own, or else he cannot hit you.

Moreover, they say that the enemy can evade these attacks by slipping and dodging. I say that he can dodge however he wishes,

---

19. Agrippa frequently refers to the inside and outside of the "cross," that is, where the two opposing blades touch. The later Italian school calls this meeting of blades *legamento*, translated by the English "engagement." It is fundamental to fencing, as one thereby gains tactile knowledge of the adversary's intentions. Later writers place great importance on this acquired sensibility, known in Italian as *tacto* and in French as *sentiment de fer*.

20. That is, the edge aligned with your knuckles when holding the sword in hand.

21. *Sforzali*. Agrippa frequently uses *forza* to refer to leverage of strong part of one's own blade on the weak part of the adversary's.

but if you attack him by moving your point all together in one action with your feet, then at the same time he moves, you can turn your right hand into high fourth, and, taking a large step to the adversary's left side with your right foot while turning your body, void your body and hit him.[22] If I haven't yet convinced you that the enemy actually winds up hurting himself, you will see it in the figure that I had made to demonstrate this, which will come in the proper order. Remember also that by turning your body in the same way, you can evade someone who closes to grapple while still threatening him with the point.

Now if someone is provoked and tries to strike with a stabbing action,[23] I say that it's a good thing for you that he has decided to so disadvantage himself. When he draws his arm back, merely lower your hand from first to second, evade his point,[24] and when you see him making his thrust, attack him with opposition.

If you want to defend against a cut to the arm, then at the same time the enemy makes the cut, turn your hand into fourth, extend your arm, and make a thrust. Also, when he attacks, you can lower your body, move your arm backwards, and not moving from first any, except to lower your point, you can interrupt his action. From there, you can make whatever cut you think is best.[25] How to make these cuts from all the guards will be explained in the proper place.

Having discussed all the whys and wherefores that I said I would, I don't think it necessary to discuss all the other types of cuts, such as *mandritti*, *riversi*, and *stramazzoni* that you can make when you are in first and someone tries to beat or seize your sword, since they are common knowledge. Therefore, let me end the discussion of the first guard by saying it is better, according to my reckoning, to defend yourself with your feet close together than from a medium stance, as I have explained above. In order to prove

---

22. See 2.3. Agrippa often tells us to move "in the same time" as the enemy.
23. That is, by drawing his hand back to strike as with a fist or blunt object.
24. That is, disengage.
25. That is, the (modern) parry of first, followed by a cut from the elbow or wrist to whichever line one wishes.

this, I have discussed both ways of defending yourself when in first — theirs, and mine, in which the feet are kept close together.

Chapter 5

Concerning the Second Guard Denoted by B

Now that you have seen how to use the first guard with the narrow stance in both defensive and offensive actions, you will surely agree that it is safer and more useful than going on guard with a wide or medium stance.[26] We therefore turn to the use of the second guard in offense and defense, which is denoted by the letter B and depicted below in its own figure [Fig. 9]. Although this guard seems to be similar to the first, because it is made by merely lowering the sword-hand a little, they are not the same because of the reasons that I will explain below. Therefore, pay careful attention to the differences between them.

First, however, I shall discuss the opinion of those who say that you ought to go on guard in second with a wide or medium space between your feet, with your sword-arm behind you, and who disparage those who use a narrow stance with their arms in front. Repeating what I said above about the first guard, if you go on guard in second, the adversary cannot attack on the outside of the engagement with the false edge.[27] Moreover, if he attacks to the inside by pressing the point of your sword with his true edge,[28] his arm will form a crescent, thus uncovering his chest, shoulder, and right knee so that they can be hit. Because of this you can, by paying close attention to time and countertime, easily hit him without being hit yourself by extending in third or fourth and then quickly going back in narrow first, even if you are smaller

---

26. *Mezzo paso*, also "half-step" or "medium pace."
27. Again, *di croce*. The false edge is that facing inwards when holding the sword in hand.
28. That is, by opposition in fourth.

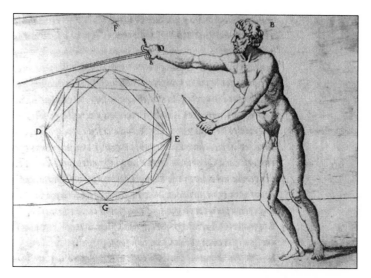

Fig. 9. The Second Guard (B).

than he is. You defend yourself so well by this that if the adversary tries to counterattack with another thrust, he will not gain even a *palmo* of distance.

And if you are on guard in narrow second and the adversary makes a long or short feint with his point or edge, you will be able to hit him, even if not with the point of the sword, without moving your left foot. Similarly, by extending your arm and quickly moving your body and foot in one action, you will be twice as quick and can steal the time from him,[29] and ruining his plans, hit him with the point. If the adversary, scorning the danger, still tries to give you a thrust under your hand when you are in second, then in order to evade his attack and hit him, step back in fourth, and if you oppose his point at the same time that you move your body, he will impale himself on your sword.[30]

---

29. Literally, *l'un doppo l'alto,* "the one double the other."
30. That is, a counterthrust in fourth while stepping back, opposing the weak part of the adversary's sword with the strong part of one's own—a technique still used in Italian fencing.

He might try to do the same thing by making a traverse step with his left foot and trying to beat your point up with his dagger, his left hand, or his arm. In that case, avoid the beat by disengaging your point to the outside, and in the same action, take a traverse step to his left side with your left foot. If you step with your left foot close to your right and keep your sword in fourth, then you will remain defended while still threatening the adversary.

CHAPTER 6

CONCERNING THE THIRD GUARD DENOTED BY C

Even though we have finished the discussion of the second guard with the narrow stance, we will still discuss its application later on, following the promised order. We now come to how to use the third guard in offense and defense.

If you are on guard in second with your feet close together and the enemy is so close that you need to move back quickly, then you should extend in fourth while moving your left foot backwards.[31] By doing this, you take yourself out of thrusting distance. You should similarly go on guard in third with a wide stance, as you can see in the figure [Fig. 10]. If the enemy is out of distance, then you ought to extend your arm when you advance or retreat in fourth or wide third, just as you do in first. Not lowering your hand and arm covers your body as much as possible, makes a stronger attack, and gives you the ability to quickly return in third. The main difference between fourth and third is that fourth is formed with a wide stance, with the right hand and arm inside the right knee and the left hand above the head, while third is made with your hand and arm held in the same way but outside the knee and your left hand in front of your chest.

---

31. That is, going into a wide stance.

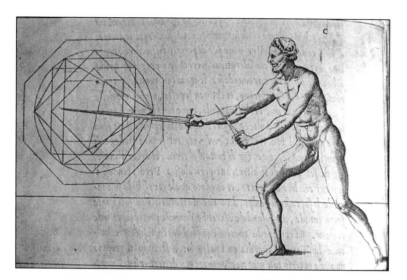

Fig. 10. The Third Guard (C).

Some of this vocation[32] say that the third guard would be bet-ter and more secure if the body was held erect, the feet a medium distance apart, and the sword arm to the rear, near the outside of the knee. I respond that, according to my reckoning, you should modify your actions according to the circumstances. Therefore, even though you do sometimes close with the enemy in the man-ner they advocate, this is not the ordinary and true principle and they err greatly in insisting that it is.

Nevertheless, as I said before, by going on guard in wide third you can at your pleasure step forwards a half-*palmo* with the right foot while keeping your left foot firm, moving your body forwards so that your right shoulder is perpendicular over your knee, and so thrust against the enemy with the advantage of more than three *palmi* of reach. Do this, as I said before, with time and

32. By "some of this vocation" (*alcuni de questa professione*), Agrippa possibly refers to professional fencing masters, whose opinion he often takes issue with.

countertime when you are on guard in third in a medium stance, in the middle of his action when he steps forward to attack with his hand close to his knee, thus interrupting his attack, hitting him with the aforesaid advantage of reach, and recovering in first or second without being hit yourself. If he tries to thrust, I say he will not succeed, since his step will be so long that he will not be able to either go forwards or recover as he normally does. However, if he tries it anyway, because of the distance between the two of you, you can give him a thrust in first or second and hit because of his disorder.

If the adversary tries to use the long step with his right foot against you, then at the same time that he moves, give him a thrust to his knee and recover as above where you made the action to hit him. If he tries to raise his right hand to attack in first or second (using the method adhered to by those others), then at the same time that he begins to move his hand, give him a thrust to the chest without moving your foot. If the enemy tries to answer this,[33] he will not be able to do so, for even if he moves his left foot up against his right to gain distance, you can do the same thing. If he tries to grab the point of the sword with his hand, you can easily lower it or move your arm backwards so that he has to come forwards to make his attack, whereupon you can easily respond in first or second and hit him with a thrust.

Though he can try in different ways to goad you into moving with the point of his sword or beat your blade with his false edge with *strammazzoni, mandritti,* and other *riversi,* both from high to low or from low to high, as well as feint cuts and thrusts to the hand or the inside or outside of the arm, you can defend against these actions by pulling your arm back, lowering the point of your sword close to your right foot, and so spoil his plans. Then, you can follow up and hit him by simply extending only your arm and your body, as above, or else try to provoke him into doing something

---

33. *Risposta,* etymologically akin to the English "riposte," but not used here in quite the same sense. In this period, the *riposto* is *any* response, not a thrust or cut that follows a parry.

with your point. A man of smaller stature who does this in first or second is safe unless the adversary is very much larger than he is.

If the enemy sees that his beat or other blow is not effective and follows up by trying to cut a *mandritto* or *riverso*, you can defend with the cross[34] and then thrust, or defend in first and thrust from below or from above, depending on where he is strong. If the enemy tries to cut from high to low, then if you quickly thrust, you will both lessen the force of his attack and have a better response.

Similarly, there are many ways to enter by *forza*.[35] For instance, if you are engaged[36] with the enemy at the middle of the swords in wide third and he tries to attack on the outside by *forza* in order to give you a thrust in the chest, change from third into narrow second and, immediately after his blow passes by, thrust in third or wide fourth.[37] If the enemy gains distance by moving his left foot close to his right[38] and tries to ride in on your sword all in action, entering on the outside by *forza*, quickly return to narrow second and then push a thrust at him, ending the action in third or fourth. If you want to send your point over his sword in third, step forward to his right side at that very moment with your left foot, opposing his blade, and in one continuous action, enter by *forza* and hit in second or third. If you are smaller or weaker than he is, then don't step forward, but rather stop him by quickly turning the point of your sword to aim at his left knee or flank. If, however, you are the larger and stronger one and he tries to do this to you, keep him covered with your point while stepping back in second with

---

34. That is, by deviating the adversary's steel by crossing it with one's own.
35. Agrippa writes *forza di arme*, which one would be tempted to translate as "force of arms," but here with the specific technical meaning of an attack with opposition. Note that while a *botta sforzata*, or expulsion, is a specific action in the classical Italian school, Agrippa's *forza* is something quite different—thrusting while opposing the weak of the adversary's sword with the strong of one's own. Agrippa does not give explicit directions for this, but the proper technique is made clear in context.
36. *Contrastando* —"standing against."
37. That is, move your right foot from a narrow stance to a wide one.
38. That is, attacks with the gain on the lunge (or "inverse advance").

your left shoulder in front, and, following his sword with your left hand as he steps, quickly give him a thrust to the chest. It is better to attack him this way because then you can choose whether or not to add this third step: the first step finds him; with the second, you advance with your left foot; and with the third you hit him, as you had intended to from the start.

I have told you how to enter on the outside by *forza* and will now tell how to enter on the inside. If you are in wide third and the enemy tries to make a short or long attack by *forza*, don't oppose him in the same way because it could lead to grappling or you might be hit in the right knee. Instead, withdraw in narrow second, and you will be safe from his attack since he can not lengthen a short attack and a long one will pass off to your right, after which you can counterattack. Most professionals don't think this is a good technique, saying that to have the point pass too close to you is dangerous. Instead, they say, you should defend by *forza* and then cut with *riverso* to the leg or head, or make a *stramazzone* or *mandritto* to the head. I respond that their technique is appropriate when faced with some brutish or unlearned person who either does not know or does not care about important techniques such as feints, half-blows, the various turns and rotations of the hand, following with the left foot, kicks, making a thrust and then throwing the adversary to the ground, twisting the weapon, and other dangerous actions. However, if you are fighting with a skilled man who has been well-taught and knows how to use these techniques, a defense such as they advocate will not only be useless to you, but useful to him.

This concludes the discussion of the third guard with a wide stance. According to my reckoning, it gives you a great advantage both in offense and defense, to the contrary of those who prefer third with the medium stance. We will discuss it further, for the substance and source of this exercise is founded in this narrow third. However, now it is time to discuss the fourth guard with the wide stance.

CHAPTER 7

CONCERNING THE FOURTH GUARD

There is little difference between the fourth guard and the third, as they are both used to keep the enemy at a distance and are very secure for defending yourself. However, the fourth is wider and more cautious than the third. You therefore go on guard in fourth differently, with your left hand over your head and your right flank forwards, not opening up your chest as you do in third. We will, therefore, not discuss what those abovementioned people think, which is that you should go on guard in fourth with a medium stance, with your right arm extended and inside your knee, opening up your chest, and sometimes holding the point of the sword high and sometimes low, with your left hand in front of the chest, ready to parry. My first guard, A, does the same job in those situations where you would use this guard. These people do not follow the true principles, nor, as I said above, do they pay proper attention to how much skill, experience, and judgment the enemy

Fig. 11. The Fourth Guard (D).

possesses. Therefore, for all the attacks we have already discussed, go on guard in wide third, and if he is skilled, avoid using this wide fourth. Rather, use the same attacks and responses[39] that we have already discussed.

After discussing various types of defense, demonstrated the four primary guards, and explaining how to practice and apply them for self-defense, I will now explain offense. The guards' versatility therein is why I believe this style is so good and advantageous. For example, if you are smaller than your adversary and you go on guard in fourth with a wide stance, you can feint to his right shoulder or his knee. When he goes to defend, disengage by lowering your sword and give him a superficial wound, returning quickly to narrow second in case he counterattacks. Then, without moving, you can repeat the feint with the point, while advancing your left foot,[40] at the same time beating his point with your left hand as you go in to attack him. If in that moment he tries to defend, disengage beneath his sword and step forwards, attacking with a thrust.[41]

If, however, you are the same size or bigger and stronger than he is, you can induce him to attack in different ways. For instance, feign letting your guard down.[42] When he goes to attack, quickly step back in second and, without pausing, thrust anew to wound him. If you don't want to let your guard down, you can beat down the point of his sword. Then, all in one action, accompanied by your left foot,[43] raise your hand into second, and, without moving at all, push a thrust as far as you can in second with your hand in fourth without moving your rear foot.[44]

---

39. *Risposte.*
40. That is, moving the left foot up against the right so as to gain distance on the "extraordinary step."
41. In other words, a disengagement made in the time of the enemy's motion, followed by an attack (bearing in mind that the "step" can be either an advance or Agrippa's "extraordinary" step).
42. Literally, *disordinasse*, "disorder one's self."
43. Again, the left foot moves up against the right.
44. What the later Italian school would call *seconda mano in quarta*. Agrippa literally say to thrust a "firm" *(firma)* Second, meaning to keep the rear foot

If you should find yourself so far from the enemy that you can't hit him, you can move a step closer to him by stepping forward towards his right side with your left foot, beating his sword with your own, and raising your hand in second. If he tries to defend, you can still push by *forza* in second and follow this with a grapple.[45] If he does not defend by jumping backwards, follow him with the point in second or fourth. I will explain how to perform this action from this guard at the proper time.

---

fixed while taking an "extraordinary" step, as in the description of the attack in the previous chapter. Certain thrusts are similarly described as "firm" throughout the work; this has been contextually manintained or translated into English as the instruction "not to move your rear foot."

45.   *Presa* (pl. *prese*). These are the grappling and infighting techniques.

CHAPTER 9[46]

CONCERNING THE SECOND GUARD DENOTED BY E

Since we have now discussed the primary guards and the offensive and defensive actions that are used with them, we ought to follow the order that I promised earlier and discuss the single figures that depict the other guards. However, you might be wondering whether in a fight you should watch your enemy's hands or his feet. My opinion is that it is best to watch his sword-hand, since the most dangerous and closest [47] attacks come from there. By going on guard in third with a wide stance, you keep the enemy so far away that he can't touch you. If he tries to press down your sword by *forza*, pull your hand back as in this figure. Note that the sword is foreshortened in the hand and does not appear because the figure is depicted standing in perspective in a wide guard.

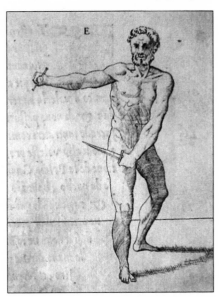

Fig. 12. The Second Guard (E).

---

46. There is no chapter 8. The original's misnumbering is preserved here.
47. And therefore quickest.

CHAPTER 10

CONCERNING THIRD GUARD WITH THE NARROW STANCE DENOTED BY F

If you step back on guard in second, then you can feint a thrust as far forward as possible while simultaneously moving your left foot up against your right. If the enemy tries to beat your sword with his left hand, make a disengagement in time and step forwards to attack him in second. You can also provoke him into moving with the various offensive actions discussed under the first guard — though you perform them differently, since before I was discussing using the actions defensively, whereas now I am discussing how to use them offensively.

In any case, recover from this action in wide third, pull your hand back toward your right knee, extend your arm to feint a thrust, and, moving your left foot up against your right, go into in narrow third, holding your right arm as in the following figure.

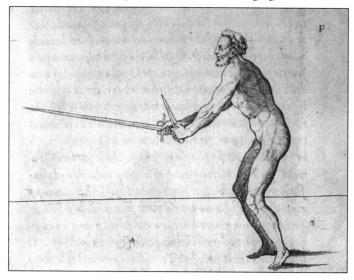

Fig. 13. The Third Guard with the Narrow Stance (F).

CHAPTER 11

CONCERNING THE ACTION DENOTED BY G

If the enemy again tries to beat your sword with his left hand, then escape by stepping to the outside — that is, to his left side — while extending your arm and hitting him in second. It is better to make the thrust in second than in third, since the step does all that is necessary: a line drawn from the point of the sword held in second will find his outside,[48] since he uncovers his body by lowering his hand when he tries to beat your sword.

If, however, at the same time that you make this action,[49] the enemy tries to beat your sword with his point,[50] then evade by disengaging beneath his hilt, aim at his right side, and all in one action, step forward and raise your hand in fourth, thus wounding him above his right arm. If he turns his hand to parry, the line only hits him better, since he uncovers his outside. If he parries with his false edge, then by however much strength he uses — no matter whether it is upwards, downwards, to the inside, or to the outside — by an equal amount will he make your attack stronger. I will explain how and why this is so in the proper place.

And if you are on guard in third with a wide stance, withdraw your sword-hand towards your knee as above and, in one action, move your left foot up against the right, make an attack to the enemy's outside — that is to the right side of his body — and send your sword over his by *forza*. If he disengages or deceives your attempt to engage, step quickly from the line of engagement with your right foot toward his left side,[51]

---

48. *Superficie*, literally the "outside of any thing" (Florio) or the circumference of a circle (considering the adversary's body as a sphere). What Agrippa means here is the part of the adversary he has uncovered by moving his hand. We have translated this as "outside" to avoid confusion.
49. *Finta*, or feint.
50. That is, actually the part of the blade near the point, where the center of percussion is located. Agrippa actually says *battarli di croce*, since the blades "cross" when doing this.
51. *[S]e pur' il ne... sfalsasse l'arma, Questo passarebbe subido di croce col pie dritto*. It is the step from the "cross" that takes one away from danger.

Fig. 14. Action G.

and voiding your *vita*,[52] move your left foot to hit him in high fourth. This is shown in the next figure, which has lines drawn back from the two points of the eyes to demonstrate that the eyes, although they are two, cannot look in more than one place at a time. Nor do they naturally travel in parallel lines, but rather finish in only one point, like a pyramid.[53]

---

52. *Vita* literally means "waist," but carries the connotation of "center of mass" (as in the Japanese *hara*) or "life." In this counterattack, Agrippa is instructing us to void or twist our center of mass away from the oncoming point, as in the later *volte* of the French school. In the milieu of sixteenth-century Rome, such an action would inevitably recall the aesthetic ideal of *contrapposto* derived from Myron's Discobolos, and which is so well displayed in the figures on the Sistine ceiling, as well as Aristotle's view of rotation as the primary form of locomotion (*Physics* VIII, 9). Interestingly, in the previous century, Alberti, in his critical writings on art (*Della Pitura* 96–97, for instance) denigrates figures that seem to be fencers! For all of these reasons and connotations — the martial, the art-historical, and the metaphorical — we have thus left *vita* untranslated.
53. Agrippa uses this optical metaphor to explain that the opposing sword, like a Galenic eye-ray, cannot but travel in a line, and so by stepping off this line of direction, the fencer secures himself from the oncoming steel.

CHAPTER 12

CONCERNING THE SECOND GUARD WITH A WIDE STANCE DENOTED BY H

If you are on guard in second in a wide stance, as in the following figure, and the enemy is in third, also in a wide stance, lower your hand and bring it back, as you did above from third, and make a feint to his right arm while, at the same time, moving your left foot up against your right. When he brings his arm back, follow him by turning your hand into fourth while stepping forward and thus go in to attack him.

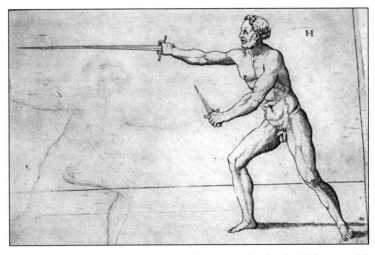

Fig. 15. The Second Guard with a Wide Stance (H).

CHAPTER 13

CONCERNING THE ACTION DENOTED BY I

If the enemy goes on guard against you in narrow third and holds his hand very far away, do this: finish your feint with an edge-blow on his sword and hit him in fourth as above, making your attack as in the following figure.[54]

Fig. 16. Action I.

---

54. In other words, a beat attack or perhaps an expulsion. Note that in the figure, the fencer's face is turned to the rear — a sensible procedure for practice in an age before masks, though one that will tend to make the attack waver at the last moment.

CHAPTER 14

CONCERNING THE ACTION INDICATED BY K

Suppose you both go on guard in a narrow stance and, at the same moment that you make your feint, the enemy thrusts on the inside of the cross in countertime. In this case, quickly raise your sword-hand in second, lower your head and body to your left side, and place your left hand on your right shoulder to accompany your thrust as you step to the enemy's right side with your right foot, as shown in the following figure. He will impale himself in that instant because his sword presses itself against yours and gives way to it, as above, and passes outside and above your right arm.[55]

Fig. 17. Action K.

---

55.   There are two different versions of the figure illustrating this action in different editions of the Blado Agrippa, one showing a very radical step to the right with the torso twisting around and the face averted. The other shows a more frontal position and the eyes facing the enemy. This better accords with the application of the technique as shown in the second part.

K

Fig. 18. Alternate
Engraving of
Action K.

CHAPTER 15

CONCERNING THE FOURTH GUARD WITH THE WIDE STANCE
DENOTED BY D

If you go on guard in fourth — the last of the four primary
guards — with a wide stance, and the enemy is in a narrow stance
in second or first, then in order to provoke and attack him, you
should extend your arm, body, and right foot as far forward as you
can — as was explained in the chapter on third guard — aiming
at his chest, and wait for his response. In order to nullify whatever
action the enemy makes in response,[56] go into second and quickly

---

56. The term Agrippa uses, *scaricare*, means to "discharge." What is
happening here is that one provokes the enemy into moving by launching an
attack that is not intended to land, but rather to provoke a response, and then
using the time he makes in responding to land one's own thrust in second
(B) before he can complete the action. In other words, it is countertime in
the modern sense.

go to hit him in the manner explained above where you do the same thing in third as a defensive action.

Fig. 19. The Fourth Guard with the Wide Stance (D)

CHAPTER 16

CONCERNING THE THIRD GUARD WITH THE NARROW
STANCE DENOTED BY L

If the enemy does not thrust, go forward into a narrow stance in third, as in the following figure. When you do this, the enemy will quickly come in and be as close as he would be if you were engaged at the middle of your swords, although your weapons will not be touching.[57]

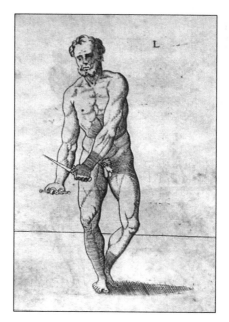

Fig. 20 The Third Guard with the Narrow Stance (L).

---

57. In other words, one withdraws one's own sword to lure in the enemy. This type of maneuver can be rather dangerous if one does not pay proper attention to measure! (Note also that Agrippa assumes blade contact will be the norm.)

CHAPTER 17

CONCERNING THE ACTION DENOTED BY G

If the enemy makes an *imbroccata* against you while keeping his rear foot firm,[58] then at the same time that he thrusts, you should turn your body as in the following figure. Because of the way you turn, step to the right, and raise your hand into high fourth, the enemy will impale himself on the sword with his outside.[59] Furthermore, you take yourself off his line — that is, away from his sword — because of the way you void your *vita*.

If, on the other hand, you were to go into third, as above, I don't believe that you could hit him because his left hand would

Fig. 21. Action G.

---

58. Again, *firma*, i.e., thrusting with the "extraordinary step" while keeping the foot firm, as before.
59. Again, *superficie*, the "outside of a thing," or, rather, the part the enemy uncovers.

beat down your point of its own accord. However, by using the action described above you can hit him in fourth over his sword.

If, however, he does not thrust, you can slip forwards and change to third, as you did above when you were threatened. Then, without waiting or losing any time, attack him in fourth.

If anyone thinks that this might be a risky and dangerous action that should not be taught,[60] I say that a man of honor well understands the techniques and tactics that he needs to use in a formal or an informal challenge.[61] Therefore, no one should complain about the risk or danger. Though I had not originally intended to mention it, let me note here that one often places oneself at risk of being hit by insignificant blows in order to emerge the victor and kill the other combatant. Accordingly, you should learn how to void your *vita*, use your unarmed hand, make attacks in time and countertime and understand the importance of the points, lines, circumferences, and surfaces.

---

60. Agrippa says, literally, *fore di ordinaria disciplina*, "outside ordinary discipline."

61. Literally, *in steccati, overo in altri lochi dove si ritrovano provocati* "in a closed field or other place where one goes when challenged."

CHAPTER 18

CONCERNING THE THIRD GUARD WITH A WIDE STANCE
DENOTED BY C

Now, suppose that you need to go on guard in third with a wide stance as in this figure, that the enemy is standing in third or fourth with a narrow stance and that your swords are touching. You can make a thrust against him, finishing in first, and beat his point down with your left hand as you step forward. In this way, you will vanquish him. Finish the action in fourth with a wide stance and then step back in second with a narrow stance.[62]

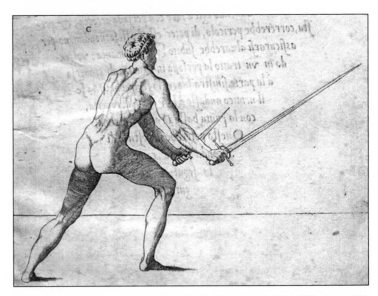

Fig. 22. The Third Guard with a Wide Stance (C).

---

62. Note the importance of blade contact in finding the enemy's sword to make the beat with the hand.

CHAPTER 19

CONCERNING THE SECOND GUARD WITH A WIDE STANCE DENOTED BY H

If the enemy thrusts at your left shoulder at the same moment that you do the above action in first, then you should realize that you are dealing with a well-practiced, agile individual and that you should defend yourself, since you are in danger of being harmed. Therefore, quickly raise your left hand and, all in one action, turn your body into fourth, step to the left side, and hit him. If, however, the enemy performs a covering parry in first with his point low, you can attack him in second without moving your rear foot, as in the following figure.

Fig. 23. The Second Guard with a Wide Stance (H).

CHAPTER 20

CONCERNING THE FIRST GUARD DENOTED BY A

If you thrust at the enemy in an arc in order to uncover his outside, you can follow up by stepping forward with your left foot and taking hold of his right arm with your left hand at the same time. This is demonstrated in the section on grappling. Note that this technique might come from this action or from others.

However, if the enemy is so quick that he can make a *stramazzone* to your head, abandon the first technique, parry him close to your hilt, and follow with the same grappling technique, raising your right hand and aiming the point at his right side in second so that he has to parry — whereupon you can attack him with a *riverso* to the flank or leg. If he doesn't parry your second, he is

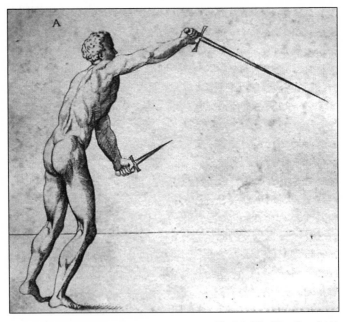

Fig. 24. The First Guard (A).

still in great danger, since you can still thrust and hit him. This is because he remains threatened by the point of your sword, which simultaneously covers your body and closes the line to hit him by *forza*. Therefore, in conclusion I say that the tumult of the crowd of critics and the plethora of opinions concerning this exercise are most tiresome. Each one is supposedly the right one because it is in common use, which leads one to conclude that this art depends as much on the judgment of Fortune as it does on proper practice.

If you are on guard in first, as in the following figure, and the enemy is in third or fourth with a wide stance and is so far away that you cannot reach him by thrusting, in order to approach him you should lower your point. If, because of the distance, he doesn't take care to guard himself, then all at once close the measure in the low line, extending forward in narrow second, beating the point in one action, and hitting him by quickly thrusting in second without moving your rear foot.[63] If he doesn't jump backward, but only draws back, follow in fourth in order to extend as far forward as you can and thus make a better attack. If he tries to parry with his sword, you can still thrust by *forza*, stepping with your left foot in order to use the above-mentioned grappling technique. If, however, you are armed with a dagger in your left hand and the enemy is stronger than you, then instead of grappling, you should make a thrust with the dagger in a single action and jump back in first.

If he tries to attack in first while you are lowering your hand, then to defend yourself step back in first or second. You can still wound him in the same time that he thrusts — no matter whether he does it by *forza* or without contact[64]—by going into fourth and striking up against his blow with the false or true edge to move his point on the outside and then immediately thrusting in second by *forza*. You can do the same thing against a *mandritto* or *stramazzone*. However, cutting to the head or leg is useless since the enemy can

---

63. Again, a "firm" second; the rear foot remains still with the "extraordinary step" carrying the blade forward.
64. *Lanciata*, literally like a spear-thrust. Leoni (2005) translates this as "flinging" the sword.

parry at the same time that you make the attack. This is the reason why I always say that you should avoid parrying unless otherwise compelled to, and instead slip, dodge, and withdraw your body, make counter-steps forward, backward, or sideways, and beat the sword away with your left hand according to the sort of attack with which you are faced.

CHAPTER 21

CONCERNING THE SECOND GUARD DENOTED BY B

Suppose you and your enemy are both on guard in second, as in the following figure, and that you are so close that both of you can hit by simply thrusting. In this case, when the enemy moves to attack, quickly void your body, step across to his left side, and

Fig. 25. The Second Guard (B).

gain the advantage by thrusting while his right foot is in the air and his sword hangs in empty space. Because of the circular motion made by your bodies, you can put your point in the same place the enemy was aiming at in a straight line.[65] If the enemy comes forward to attack with his sword, respond by holding your hand low so that if you need to, you can parry him by raising your hand while voiding your *vita*, as previously discussed, and hit him by remaining in high fourth and aiming at his left side.

If both of you are on guard in second at the same distance as above, but the enemy does not make the first move, lower your sword, engaging his on the inside so that they touch.[66] Some might argue against this, saying that enemy could disengage and make a strong thrust at your chest. However, I say that in this case, you ought to deliberately make this action in order to cause him to move, and at the same time that he thrusts above your sword on the outside, counterattack beneath his weapon in fourth and hit him while ceding your body.

CHAPTER 22

CONCERNING THE ACTION DENOTED BY I

Suppose you and your enemy are both in second as above, and he feints a thrust in second and quickly turns a *stramazzone* to your head. You could perhaps step back with a cut as he attacks, parrying crosswise by *forza* — which will be discussed separately— and then come in to use a grappling technique — which requires a great deal of effort and skill, though it should still be used depending on

---

65. Again considering the body, and one's personal space, as a sphere. We see here glimmerings of the Spanish school of fencing developed by Jeronimo de Carranza in the 1560s.

66. Literally, "crossing." Though Agrippa does not explicitly discuss the engagement (later termed *legamento* in the Italian school), it is again clear from actions such as this and his use of blade contact that it is an important technique in his fencing

Fig. 26. Action I.

the situation and the adversary. However, since you are on guard
in second, all you have to do is make a thrust against him at the
same time that he moves while moving your left foot backward so
that you are in fourth as in the following figure. Thus, by hardly
moving you will both hit him in the chest and remain safe.

    To counter anyone who says that an enemy in a guard similar
to second can do the same thing to you, I say that he will be too
far away because of the way he lowers his point and shoulder
when he thrusts to your low line. Also, by stepping back and
withdrawing your body, you can create an opportunity to either
hit the adversary in his right shoulder, however lightly, and so ruin
his plans and be able to counterattack, or else, because you void
your *vita* by stepping back, you can also stop him with your point
as explained above.

Chapter 23

Concerning the Action Denoted by K

If the two of you are in second in the same situation as above, then quickly find the enemy's sword with yours, again engaging the blade on the outside. If the enemy thrusts at the same time that you move your sword, then without raising or evading his weapon, you can easily hit him in countertime because of the number of the motion he has made.[67] This is a very important technique. Although some say that you are safe from harm if you oppose the enemy's sword, pushing with your edge on the outside, I counter that this is more

Fig. 27.
Action
K.

67. This passage makes clear Agrippa's Aristotelian conception of time as motion and stillness; time is measured by the "number of the motion" of the weapon (*Physics*, IV). Fencer A's engagement creates one time, Fencer B uses that time to reply with a thrust, and Fencer A moves against (or counter) to that time with his counterthrust.

dangerous. If you resist and push on the outside, then your sword will quickly slide down against his hilt — where it exerts the least amount of force — and you will expose the outside of your chest to his blade, and moreover, will not be able to escape an attempt to grapple without risk and disadvantage.

Therefore, you ought not to parry in this way, but rather defend yourself using the following method. This is, according to my judgment, both sufficiently secure and valuable not only to those who are as big and strong as the adversary, but also, as I said above, to those who are smaller. When the enemy makes the sudden thrust as above, then in the same time, aim your sword at his right side in second, and, accompanying the enemy's sword with your left hand, step with your right foot to his left side, supporting your chin on your left shoulder and casting your eyes to the ground.[68] This technique is seen in the following figure and should be done quickly and in one movement. It not only pushes the thrust into the enemy's chest, but also agilely voids and lowers your body, thus giving the weaker man a certain and sure advantage. For these reasons, it seems to me to be a most logical technique.[69]

Note that though the following figure seems to be holding only the hilt, the sword is shown in profile just like the one noted above where the sword is being held in a similar way.

CHAPTER 24

CONCERNING THE THIRD GUARD WITH A NARROW STANCE DENOTED BY F

Because all arts and exercises ought to be complete, I wish to verify and corroborate this discussion with examples. I therefore introduce the present example, which concerns the methods I have proposed to avoid attacks, cede your body, void your *vita*, and set a lesser force

---

68. Note also the position of the figure is similar to the Belvedere Torso.
69. Literally, "a most true reason," again equating the fencing bout with a logical proof.

against a greater and so defend yourself against a stronger man —
essentially, how to choose intelligently the less risky course of action
when you are forced into a dangerous situation. You can see the
proof of this with a ball, as in the following figure.[70] Imagine you
were to place the ball on the ground and if you try to strike it in
whatever way you can, and on whatever side you wish to, you can
well imagine that you will not be able to strike it firmly, no matter
whether you hit it in the center or on the edge.[71] This is because
it defends itself by moving. In fact, if you study how it moves, you
will see that it is a naturally mobile instrument.

It therefore seems to me that this is a model for our bodies,
which are not like balls in what they are made of, but rather in how
they move. You can understand everything you need to know to use
the techniques I have discussed if you remember that our bodies
are the same as the ball and move with the same skill and agility.
Therefore, no one should make this task impossible for themselves
by thinking it strange or difficult, for, as I have said before, it is not.
If an insensate thing placed in a field instinctively gives way to a
blow and defends itself by naturally moving the striking imple-
ment outside its body from one side to the other with the same
part that is struck, rolling forward and back and sideways and every
which way, then how much better do our trained bodies do the
same — according to the place, time, and situation — in order to
attack the enemy and defend ourselves from him? The same thing
is true for voiding the *vita* and similar actions, according to the
admonitions that should prevail when you are forced to use the
art. It is in this that the sole advantage of practicing the art rests.
The rest is subject to the whims of Fortune, insofar as it is possible
for a reasoned approach for the use of arms to complement your
own strength, as has been shown.

---

70. Agrippa says *esperienza*, "experience" or "experiment." Following the
standard (Aquinan) ontological model, we have true knowledge of a thing
through our mental experience and reflection thereon.
71. Agrippa literally says, "on the diameter, going against the radius."

Fig. 28. The Third Guard with a Narrow Stance (F) and a Ball.

To give an example of these principles, let me explain that the body of this figure is firm only on its right foot, aided and supported by the point of the left, not fixed, but rather like an axis,[72] similar to how a ball rolls after being pushed or otherwise disturbed. Although I explained above in the descriptions of the guards how to void the *vita* or body, I did not previously mention this. However, it can be proven by opposing the enemy's weapon with your own. This action shows that the true and ordinary principles cause us to move in a way that allows our bodies to evade and give way from the enemy's blows, just as the ball does. This is because when the enemy tries to attack by opposing your sword on the outside by *forza*, you can simply turn your body without moving at all from your original position, thus showing your right flank, and turn your hand into high fourth while keeping the point directed at the adversary. In this way he will, as already said, impale himself on your sword, and you will escape without

---

72. In the sense of a locus of motion about which one moves.

harm. Thereby is seen certain proof that whoever is stronger and has the more powerful body will demonstrate the superiority of the smaller man every time.

If the enemy tries to enter on the inside by *forza*, then just as above, without moving, you can turn your body to the other side and, showing your left flank and go into second while aiming your point at the enemy. You do this simply by ceding to the greater force while defending yourself by turning your body, moving like the above-mentioned ball, without any doubt that the adversary will impale himself. The other reason for this is that, as already mentioned, parrying is forbidden[73] since nothing can come of it but a redoubling of the attack. As much as you resist your enemy's sword, and however you do it, then by the same amount you put yourself in danger of being hit or grappled. This is to the enemy's advantage, since he can remain unharmed while hurting you.

Other than that, by turning your body as above, you can, all in one action, move before him and so take the advantage, thus interrupting all his designs. By using this technique, you will balance the scales between you, making your enemy's plans empty and vain while yours will fully succeed. The reason for this is that you can both defend against your enemy's attacks and hit him in the shortest possible time because of the way your carry yourself and because your weight is centered over one foot. You are not as fast if you go on guard with your weight evenly distributed, since to move you need another moment of time.[74] However, the above action does not restrict your time, and is the true rule of this art. As the figure partially demonstrates, by standing in this way and using your *vita*, when the proper moment comes to harm the enemy so elegantly, you will be ready to do it without losing an instant at the moment the spirit moves you. And if anyone wants to repeat that engaging the enemy's weapon presents little obstacle to him — since he can

---

73. See page 46 above.

74. In other words, another fencing time—one to shift the weight to one foot, and the other to step. On fencing time, see, pp. lxiv–lxvi.

provoke you into moving in different ways, or he can feint, or he can make a determined thrust against you, or other similar tactics — I reply that these can be countered by the techniques that I have already mentioned, and that are discussed copiously below.

CHAPTER 25

CONCERNING ANOTHER FIRST GUARD DENOTED BY N

Now that we have sufficiently discussed the ordinary way of doing things with your right foot in front, we proceed to the discussion of the guards with the left foot in front. The general opinion concerning this is varied, with some maintaining that it is useful and advantageous to go on guard with your left foot in front, as in the following figure. My opinion, for the same reasons I gave before, is that guards of this sort are somewhat acceptable under justified and necessary circumstances. These have not been previously mentioned, but will be discussed below.

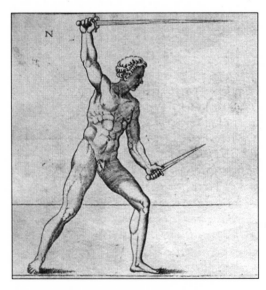

*Fig. 29. Another
First Guard
(N).*

For instance, suppose you are fighting with an enemy who is as strong as you are, with neither of you wearing armor,[75] and he goes on guard in first with his left foot in front. In this case, go on guard in ordinary fourth with a wide stance and the right foot in front and come forward to meet him in narrow third. If he does not move before you close the distance in third, thrust beneath his dagger in second. When he tries to lower the point of his dagger to parry your sword to the outside, intending to take a traverse step, he will open himself up so that he will be easy to hit.

If it should happen that you find yourself on guard in first with your left foot in front, turn your left shoulder to the inside, but only to evade the parry — which is forbidden for the reasons I have already given [76] — and follow[77] the enemy's sword so it passes to your outside. If he jumps back, follow him with a right *imbrocatta* in wide, long fourth.

CHAPTER 26

CONCERNING ANOTHER THIRD GUARD DENOTED BY O

If your enemy goes on guard in third with his left foot in front, as in the following figure, then without losing any time, just as above, come in to meet him in ordinary narrow third with your right foot in front and the point of your sword close to the ground so that the enemy cannot beat it or raise it with the dagger. Standing in this way, you can, without losing a moment of time, send your point over the adversary's dagger so that he will try to parry upwards with the dagger while taking a counter-step to attack with his sword. However, you immediately deceive the dagger, lower your point, and, all at once, take a traverse step to your right with

---

75. Literally, *in camisa*, or "in shirtsleeves"—that is, not in plate armor or a shirt of mail, as was sometimes done in formal duels.

76. See p. 46.

77. *Accompagnando*, "accompanying," giving the connotation of applying pressure to the enemy's blade.

Fig. 30. Another Third Guard (O).

your right foot — that is to the enemy's left side—and thrust in fourth to hit him in the chest. If it should happen that you can't hit him and the enemy takes his step, beat his sword upwards and to the left with a backhanded motion of your left hand. Do all of this, save for the feint going forward, in one action.

CHAPTER 27

CONCERNING ANOTHER FIRST GUARD DENOTED BY N

Since someone might ask me which of the aforesaid guards in first and third with the left foot forwards is wiser and more advantageous for attacking the enemy, I say that you can judge for yourself by putting it to the test. If the enemy is on guard with his left foot in front, you cannot easily induce him to launch an attack in any guard except first because it is too uncertain. This is because as soon as he thrusts, you can gain the advantage in one action and without feinting in the manner described above. The

*Fig. 31. Another
First Guard
(N).*

reason is that a blow from third can beat his attack up with very little force and is stronger and more advantageous than the first guard because it comes from outside the body. Knowing that as a rule the hand gives way more easily on the inside than the outside, it is very important that you oppose as much as possible with your right hand to uncover the enemy's body; on the other hand, he, by opposing upwards with his parry, only makes it easier for you to hit him. The sort of people who do this try to oppose with the half of the blade closest to the point, which is dangerous and causes the weapon to fall from their hands.

Now that I have explained my opinion concerning the two guards with the left foot in front, I want to discuss another guard that is similar to the aforementioned first. The following figure shows how the enemy can make a feint to your chest while you are on guard in fourth with a wide stance, coordinating the action with his right foot. He does this planning to make you parry upwards with your dagger, which he then deceives and hits you. Therefore, I repeat that you should not parry, because when he feints with his left foot forward his thrust will fall short unless he turns so that his right foot is forward. Knowing the imperfection and deficiency of such a feint, do not use the same technique, but instead extend as far forward as you can with your whole body and you will be able to hit him in fourth in the knee, arm, or left shoulder because he is so close. Some people might argue that he can take a quick step forward with his attack and so hit you. To satisfy them, I say that at the same time, you can step backward into narrow first, beat down the blow the enemy is trying so hard to land and hit him in first or second.

By making time and measure agree and by encountering his force on the outside, you can hit the enemy in his closest or most open place while he is still feinting and, therefore, unable to wound you. This is because he lowers his point towards his feet in order to beat your sword, whereas your line goes directly to his chest by the quickest and shortest route. This is how you should defend yourself when the enemy tries to goad you into making some sort of action.

CHAPTER 28

CONCERNING THE THIRD GUARD DENOTED BY O

If, as before, you see the enemy trying to provoke you into making some action by coming forward in third with his left foot in front as seen in the following figure, then you ought to go into third with a wide stance, holding your hand close to your knee and your dagger hand over your head. If the enemy decides to step forward to attack you resolutely, then you should retire backward in ordinary second and, beating his point to the outside with your left hand, quickly step forward with your right foot to hit him in second. Knowing that he will put himself at a disadvantage by being unable to find your sword with his own because his action is contrary to the true principles of the art, he would be wise to make various feints, accompanying his step by thrusting or by cutting *mandritti*

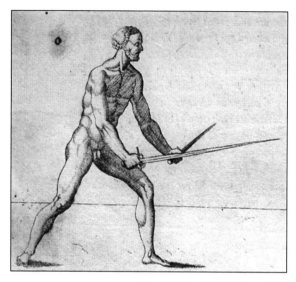

Fig. 32. Another Third Guard (O).

to the leg. However, these attacks will be in vain, since by being
in a wide stance you will not need to parry so that you will not
be deceived by his feints.[78]

Following my judgment, this wide stance is more advantageous
and profitable against experienced swordsmen, those who have not
yet learned how to fence and those low-born and uncultured men
who do not handle weapons. This was demonstrated above when
I discussed going on guard with a wide stance in third and fourth
with your right foot forward, whereby you can stop and interrupt
many plans, techniques, and actions that your enemy might try,
no matter how practiced and crafty he might be. This is because it
consists of only these actions that teach you the main part and best
knowledge of how to defend yourself and attack others. Its ability
and ease of use lie in practicing how to thrust forward, recover in
fourth guard, and extend your body as far forward as you can, as

---

78.   Literallly, *manco è sottoposto a' le finte*, "lest he be placed below the feints."

was discussed in the explanation of this guard. The same goes for defending yourself by stepping backward and going on guard in first or second with the point aimed at your enemy, and also going on guard in third with a wide stance, just as with fourth, as mentioned above. We learn this not only through discipline and practice, but also from natural caution, which teaches us to defend ourselves against attack. How much better, then, can someone perform who observes my principles? They seem to me to be legitimate, good, and profitable to anyone who adopts them, and easy for anyone to follow, no matter what kind of person[79] he might be.[80]

CHAPTER 29[81]

Here at the end of this discussion, let me recommend the two abovementioned guards to all sorts of men, both those who are well-practiced and those who are inexpert. It is my opinion that they are profitable and advantageous for all, but much more so for larger men than for smaller. I therefore ought to say something for the benefit of smaller men — that is, those who are physically weaker — so that even if they are not well-practiced, they may be well-advised.

If your enemy is bigger than you, go on guard in third with a narrow stance, like the figure with the ball. If you don't know how to evade or parry attacks, or how to void and cede your *vita* and body by stepping and traversing and the other necessary things, then when you encounter your enemy hold the point of your sword low and close to the ground, so that your opponent cannot beat it, seize it, or raise it. Wait until he tries with feints or cuts or anything else he might decide to do, to provoke you into moving

---

79. Literally, *per qual spirito si sia*, "by whatever spirit there might be."
80. Note here that the image here also differs between the two editions, with the earlier showing the figure facing to the left with its back to the viewer and the later showing the figure facing to the right. The position, however, is identical.
81. Agrippa did not number this chapter.

then, at that moment, make a thrust in fourth against him — unless he himself is on guard in fourth with a wide stance.[82]

This is because no matter how he makes the feint, whether by cut or thrust, you should respond to him as soon as he moves, since he cannot defend himself in that moment. Rather, it will be to your advantage, as the smaller man, because of the reasons discussed at the beginning of this work concerning the defensive use of the fourth and third guards.[83] This will be seen in figures 2 through 5, where the proper measure is depicted, and where you can see how to place your feet and how to apply the various techniques that have been demonstrated and annotated by letters following the order of the alphabet.[84]

---

82. That is, a thrust in countertime.
83. See pp. 22–29.
84. See pp. 65–69.

BOOK 2

I have sufficiently discussed the primary guards used in this pursuit, and also those derived from them; I have also demonstrated a number of feints, attacks, and other techniques. I have accompanied this art with the imaginative faculty by means of points, lines, times, and other terms for describing the motion of the body and the weapon according to the given principles. By means of these techniques lesser strength can conquer greater. I have thus discharged the obligation I undertook when I promised many noble, learned, and valorous men that I would show, if I could, how to perform the above-mentioned feints, attacks, and techniques demonstrated in the first part of this work.

Therefore, here begin the sequences of actions. First remember what I said: the letter A means the first, B means the second, C means the third, and D means the fourth primary guard, and that the subsequent guards and actions derived from the primaries are shown in their own figures with their own letters, as seen previously. This has been done in order to abbreviate the discussion and make my meaning clearer. Let me also mention to you that the letter signifying first, second, third, fourth, or any other guard for use in offense or defense is placed at the foot of the figure to identify them, and the letter showing the technique from which the application follows is placed at the head of the figure, so that you can understand what happens.

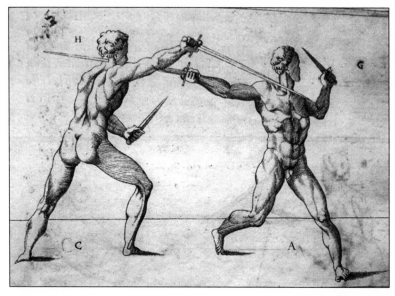

Fig. 33. Application of H vs. G.

CHAPTER 1

Turning now to the techniques, suppose someone goes on guard
in A and his enemy is in C, and the man in C wants to go into A
in order to attack the first fencer in opposition,[1] forcing his sword
down with the true edge. The first fencer should disengage over
the guard,[2] aiming at the enemy's chest, and take a large step with
his right foot to the enemy's left side. In this way he makes a circumference and a new perspective, voiding his body while hitting
the enemy in the chest as in the technique of G discussed above.[3]
If the enemy tries to follow in first, then he will impale himself
on his adversary's sword. Thus, lesser force can conquer greater, as
has been said throughout this work.

---

1. "By cross" *(di croce)*.
2. Literally, "turning the sword-hand in rotation above" *(voltando la mano
de la spada in giro di sopra)*.
3. See pp. 40–41.

CHAPTER 2

After explaining in simple terms some of the many varied techniques possible from the guards of B and C, I will now discuss their application, which is this: if a fencer on guard in C wants to attack a fencer on guard in B, the former can change his guard to B[4] and, pressing[5] on the enemy's sword, quickly follow by *forza* and give him a thrust in the chest, which does the same thing as the attack in H. The fencer on guard in B, in order to defend himself and hit

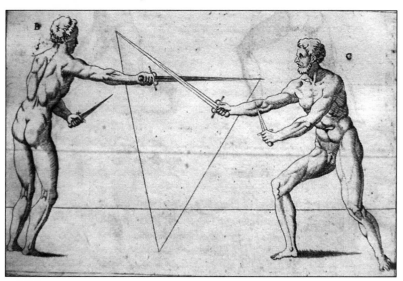

Fig. 34. Application of B vs. C.

the first fencer when he goes to attack by opposition,[6] can wound him as I have already said, perhaps with a low *riverso* or a *stramazone* to the head or a low or high *mandritto tondo*. However, the parry is dangerous, because it gives time to the enemy and presents the

---

4.   That is, the first fencer changes from third to second.
5.   *Sforzando la spada.*
6.   *Sforzarli la spada.*

risk of being grappled, which will be discussed in its proper place.[7] Therefore when fencer C makes his attack in the position of H, it would be better for the man on guard in B to disengage from the enemy's sword — or more accurately, evade[8] it — and hit him in the chest in the position of K, or place himself in the position of G, voiding his *vita*, thus making a new perspective as in the figure of G.

If the man on guard in B wants to attack the man on guard in C, then, turning his chest and pushing the sword as above, he can use the technique shown in Figure H. The fencer on guard in C can parry this and make the abovementioned cuts, that is the *riverso*, *stramazzone*, and *tondo*, but — as I have said many times — it would be better if he scorned the parry as dangerous, withdrew in the position of B, and then quickly used technique H. This is how both a man on guard in B and a man on guard in C can defend himself and attack his enemy.

So that no one is confused by the swords in the figure, since one, being obscured, seems to be longer than the other, I will prove that they are the same length. Look from the ground to the point of the sword, and observing the geometrical rule, you will find that they are not at all different because the short one is shown to be long, and the long one, short.

Chapter 3

I placed a diagram at the beginning of this treatise with straight lines and angles, inscribed with letters, an arm, and a leg in order to demonstrate a straight line and a bent one, and in the previous double figure I showed how a straight line is stronger than a bent one.[9] In another action, I will show the opposite — how a bent line can conquer a straight one, provided you observe the ordinances, methods, times, and countertimes described.

---

7.   Chapters 18–20, below.

8.   *Fuggendo la spada, o per dir meglio schifandola.* A disengagement in time.

9.   Figs. 8 and 9.

Fig. 35. Application of I vs. A.

Regarding the straight line, if two men are fighting, the one in the guard of C and the other in the guard of D, and the man in D changes to A or another guard, then, while fencer D is changing his guard, fencer C should make a thrust against him all in one time in the position of I. Thus does the straight line conquer, as you can see. This is called "countertime in favor of fencer C." In the moment the man on guard in D goes into A or another guard, C hits him in the chest or the shoulder in the position of I, gaining the advantage of reach by making a straight line,[10] while the man on guard in D falls short, since he makes an angle or, as one might say, a bent line.

10. Literally, "with such advantage of the sword" (*con tanto avantaggio di spada*).

Fig. 36. Application of A vs. D.

CHAPTER 4

Suppose in this case that the fencer on guard in D has made a feint at the arm of the fencer on guard in A in order to make him move, as in the discussion of the defense and offense of the fourth guard,[11] and that A didn't move. Fencer D can then go into the position of B and, beating the point of A's sword with his left hand, quickly thrust and hit him in the position of H. Since the fencer on guard in A might thrust at the instant that fencer D makes the feint to his arm, the latter can, just as if he had made the feint, quickly withdraw in the position of B, beat A's sword away with his hand, and attack in the position of H. This is the procedure to follow with the sword used by itself, with the sword and dagger, with the cape, with the gauntlet, with another sword in your left hand, and other weapons you can beat with.

---

11. Page 28. The feint was actually to the shoulder.

CHAPTER 5

The attack of H, which you see here being made against the person marked with the letter B, can come from the attack in F in the following manner. If a fencer on guard in C goes into B to beat with his dagger the sword of a fencer on guard in F, then the man in F can deceive the weapon and hit him in countertime in the position of H as discussed above (following the methods and purposes discussed there). Note also that similar attacks can be made against beats in the positions of A, B, and C, as well as the other guards that have been mentioned, and as we have seen, in many other ways, as well — either when the enemy tries to beat your sword, or when you give him the opportunity to beat it by making a feint.

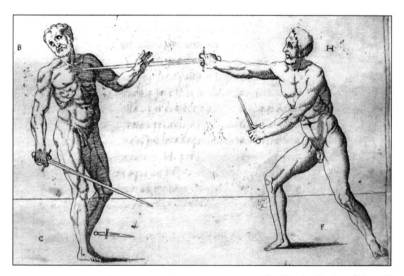

Fig. 37. Application of B vs. H.

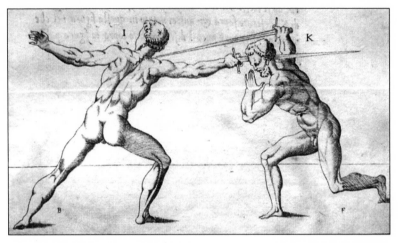

Fig. 38. Application of I vs. K.

CHAPTER 6

And because I said that I would show how a bent line could vanquish a straight one, here is the demonstration. It uses the technique of K, which you can get to from various guards, but here I will show how to do from the position of F.

If a fencer in B and a fencer in F are on guard close to each other, and the man on guard in B attacks by opposition in order to hit his adversary in the position of I,[12] the man in F cedes to his force,[13] lowering his head and body to his left side while placing his left hand on his right shoulder and all in one time, steps across toward the enemy's right side with his right foot so that the enemy impales himself on the sword, thus performing the technique of K mentioned above. This figure thus demonstrates what was said in the discussion concerning the figure placed over an axis.[14]

---

12. *Et andando B. di croce per offendere*, "goes to attack by the cross."

13. *...cedendo à quella forza*.

14. See p. 53, where the foot that does not move, which is the locus of motion, is likened to an axis, similar to how the center of the ball moves.

Fig. 39. Application of A vs. F.

CHAPTER 7

Since the regulation is that if a man touches the barrier of the lists, he loses the duel, here is, against the conventional wisdom, a remedy for the man of lesser strength.[15] Therefore, if a man of lesser strength is on guard in F close to the barrier, or fears that the enemy will beat his sword to take it on the outside, he can go on guard in L with his hand close to his knee and the point of his sword close to the ground, and wait for the enemy to place himself in the guard of A as shown here — or in another guard — in order to hit the former with an *imbroccata* in the position of H or make him, the man of lesser strength, touch the barrier in some way. At the moment he makes the thrust, the man of lesser strength can then perform the technique of F or L while voiding his body and putting it into a new perspective by stepping forward to the adversary's left side with his right foot. This will give the

---

15. See p. xl.

effect of G or P, thus allowing the fencer to escape the enemy's beat as noted above. Whenever he tries to attack with some other technique, the defenses described throughout this work will prevail, demonstrating how the lesser force can vanquish the greater with the same method shown in the first two figures marked H and G.

CHAPTER 8

And to demonstrate the harm that an ill-considered and resolute attack[16] can do, I present these two figures, marked with the same letter and possessing the same size, knowledge, and skill. Suppose they are both in the position of F at the measure of the half-sword and the first one goes to attack his enemy by entering on the outside by *forza* in the position of H. The other voids his *vita*, disengages

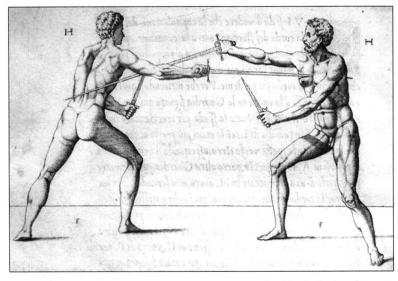

Fig. 40. Application of H vs. H.

---

16. Agrippa literally says a "provocation" (*provocatione*) though here with a degree of commitment that implies it is a real attack.

from the enemy's sword, beats it away with his left hand, and steps towards his enemy's right side with his right foot to hit him with a thrust in H, as is seen here.

CHAPTER 9

Taking into account the good advice given above to the person who was attacked, the attacker can emerge victorious if he knows this technique. After beginning to make his attack as in the last chapter, the attacker makes a small pause so that when the enemy voids his *vita* and disengages his sword to beat with his left hand and hit in the position of H, the attacker, having turned his hand, can attack him using the technique of G or P (there being no difference

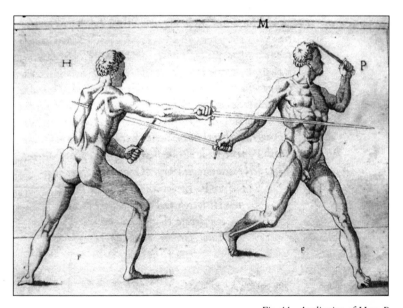

Fig. 41. Application of H vs. P.

between G and P save that in the former the arm is high and in the latter it is low).[17] Thus, a little boldness will lead to victory.[18]

CHAPTER 10

Similarly, suppose the two enemies whose movements and attacks are shown in the figure are on guard in C. (Note that the guard of C does not appear save as the letter placed by their feet, and that

Fig. 42. Sequence F–I vs. A–I.

the other guards, G and D, are explained below as the means by which the attacker or defender can hit his adversary.)

---

17. N.B. the figure in the diagram is labeled F since this is the position it *began* from.

18. Literally, "thus a well-considered presumption on the part of the attacker will make itself felt on the adversary," *(cosi quella presuntione poco considerata ch'esso provocatore usò, sarebbbe venuta ad effettuarsi ne l'aversario).* This is countertime in the modern sense.

First, if fencer C feints an attack in I against a man on guard in A, he should not complete the attack, but hold back as much as he can in order to be able to change to the guard of F, which he will see as more useful to him. Having tried to intercept his enemy before the thrust in I — which was actually a feint — could arrive, the man on guard in A will be in such disorder that he will not be able to recover to guard. When he cautiously pauses because he cannot find the blade of his enemy held in I, the first fencer, who is now in F, can hit him on the outside by making a resolute thrust in G or D while beating the enemy's sword above his right arm with his left hand.

Similarly, the other fencer on guard in C can become the initiator and first to strike by attacking the fencer in F in the same fashion. If the enemy has made the same feint in I — again not making the thrust resolutely but holding back somewhat — he can attack during the pause the attacker makes. This example clearly shows that it can be both good and bad to attack resolutely, and conversely, it can be both good and bad to hold back. This has been discussed above and will be seen again, and is due to the double considerations of points, lines, times, and countertimes.

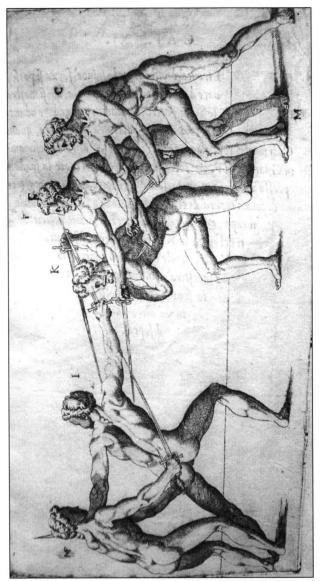

Fig. 43. Sequence F–I vs. C–C–K.

Chapter 11

In the preceding figures, we saw how a man using less strength can defend himself against a man using greater strength and thus hit his adversary. What is shown in this figure is how to set this up.[19] It proceeds in the following way. The fencer in the guard of C, who is using less strength, advances in the position of F against the other swordsman, who is also in F, and engages his sword lightly on the inside to cause[20] him to disorder himself. When his adversary, who is using more strength, attacks by opposition in the position of I,[21] then the man who is using less strength lowers his head and, doing the other things described in the technique of K, makes the thrust so that the adversary impales himself. This is seen in this present figure and is also demonstrated in another above.[22]

---

19. *Come possi andare ad incontrarla et vincere* ("how to go to meet and conquer it").

20. *Invitarlo*, though not in the same sense of an "invitation" as used in later Italian schools. In these, one positions oneself in such a way that a line is opened so that the adversary will make his attack there. Agrippa's "invitation" is a *proactive* one, causing the adversary to "disorder" himself; the latter "invitation" is *reactive*.

21. *In[t]rarà di croce in I.*

22. The illustrations for chapters 11 through 14 of Book 2 (pp. 76, 78, 80, 82) were originally fold-out inserts glued into the book.

Fig. 44. Sequence F–H vs. C–C–G.

Chapter 12

The same thing happens in the action shown here. If someone, who is on guard in C, goes into the position of F to attack someone who is also in F, but who is using more strength, he can engage him on the outside so the enemy, putting his faith in his own valor, will make a thrust in H. At that moment, the man using less strength disengages[23] beneath the enemy's sword, turning into the position of G as is seen here, or else into P. In the same way, if the man using greater strength pushes low from the guard of C, the man using less strength can disengage over the enemy's sword and make a thrust in the positions of G or P. Also, in the same time that the man who is using more strength pushes his body forward, the man using less force can disengage his sword and, beating away the adversary's weapon with his left hand, make a thrust in the position of K — unless the enemy is on guard with a target, buckler, or round-shield, in which case it is better to hit him in the position of G or P, as above.

---

23. *Sfalsando.*

Fig. 45. Sequence N–I vs. A–I.

Chapter 13

Here are two adversaries, the one on guard in N and the other on guard in C. The man on guard in C feints in the position of I to the other's knee, arm, or left shoulder, since these are closest to his sword. When the fencer on guard in N answers this by thrusting resolutely in I, his adversary can recover into the guard of A, and beating down his enemy's thrust, reply by hitting him in the position of H. The fencer on guard in N could step forward with a feint and cut a high or low *mandritto*, but because the fencer who was in C steps back in the guard of A, the low cut would miss while the enemy would impale himself on the point, since his sword will make an oblique line from his shoulder to the ground while the other held his straight. The high cut would not do any harm either, since the blow would parry itself.[24]

---

24. That is, will fall upon the sword held in A.

Fig. 46. Sequence B-I vs. O-D.

82

CHAPTER 14

When someone on guard in C wants to attack someone standing on guard in O with their left foot forward, as seen here, he can make a feint in the position of I in order to recover in the guard of B to continue on in H. At the moment when the man who was on guard in C is lowering the sword from the position of B to the position of H, the man on guard in O can reply by feinting a thrust in I and attacking in the position of D, and then recovering to B or F. From the position of B, the man who was in O can use the technique of H, or if he is in F, he can defend himself with a thrust in the positions of G or D with his sword outside his enemy's, as has been explained many times previously.

If, however, the man in O doesn't want to step into the feint of the man who was in C or use the feint of N that was discussed in the preceding chapter, the former can decide to use any feint or method I have described in this work.

Though these might seem dangerous, nonetheless a man of honor who knows the principles and how to deal with his enemy will find them valuable. Moreover, as mentioned at the beginning of this treatise, a man ought not to care a whit for any danger in pursuing his goals. Rather, we have discussed each technique by what we can observe of its properties, so that you can use the most efficient one as it pleases you. Furthermore, though they perhaps seem different, what has been said of the sword and sword and dagger also applies to all of those weapons that follow — for I have said, and say now, and will always say, that a sword alone, provided it is skillfully wielded and governed by the principles I have given, will give you the ability to use all other weapons just as an author uses all of the letters of the alphabet.

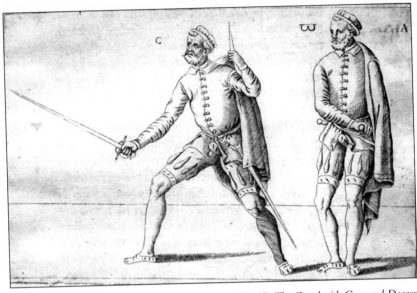

Fig. 47. The Guard with Cape and Dagger.

CHAPTER 15

Following the order laid out at the beginning of this discussion, I will now talk about how to go on guard holding the cape with the dagger.[25] Though this may seem to be a very simple thing to do and superfluous to the discourse, it is both good to know and relevant, and anyone armed with the sword, dagger, and cape who is either trying to goad someone else into fighting or who is themselves being so provoked, ought to follow this procedure no matter what situation they find themselves in.[26]

---

25. Agrippa uses the term *imbracciatura* (literally, "embracing" the cloak and dagger).

26. More so than the other sections, Agrippa seems to be referring here to "street" techniques — i.e., how to go on guard in an impromptu encounter. Certainly, using one's cloak in self-defense does not smack of a formal trial by combat!

First, extend your right arm so your cape falls from your shoulder. Then, at the same time, put one hand on your sword and the other on your dagger and go on guard in C, since if you were to go on guard in A, your cape could fall to the ground and the other guards are not as good for using the techniques I have previously discussed. Quickly drawing your sword and dagger, raise your cape from your shoulder with your dagger-hand, with the larger part of the dagger outside and to the right of the loop.[27] Bending at the waist[28] a little backward and to the left, extend your arm, making a wave with the cape to wrap it around the outside of your dagger-hand. Hold it next to your hip and you will be safe from thrusts, since you are holding the dagger and the cape as shown in the present figure. I believe going on guard[29] this way is better than doing it with the dagger or cape alone, since if some people prefer the dagger, and others the cape, I, knowing that both of them are good to use alone, reckon that it ought to be better to have both.

CHAPTER 16

Laying to rest the discussion of how to go on guard with the cloak, let me say that by going on guard with it in this way, you can use it to parry attacks to your head and leg since it protects your arm. The cloak is also good for either throwing or holding on to so that your adversary cannot use it.

We now turn to these two figures, which are the same in form and effect as the double figures discussed above. If the adversaries go on guard in A and F, and the man on guard in A does not make a low thrust at the man on guard in F, then the latter can step back in the position of D and turn his cape around his arm and, feinting a thrust at the enemy's face, beat his sword with the cape, and thrust

---

27. The *cappino*, literally, "little loop" the cloak makes when shrugged off in this manner. See the figure for details.
28. *Vita.*
29. *Questa imbracciatura.*

Fig. 48. Cape and Dagger, A vs. F.

in A or B — unless the other man hits him in countertime in the position of P while he's trying to beat the sword with the cape.

If the man in F does not move against the man in A, and the latter still wants to attack him, but is afraid to do so at that moment because he fears a thrust in G or P, he can go on guard in D while unwrapping the cape from his arm, change his guard to A, and engage the enemy's blade[30] while in the same moment throwing the cape over the straight part of the sword of the man in F,[31] and then, all in one time, hit his adversary by thrusting in H — unless in the moment he engages the sword of the man in F, the latter turns his hand on high and hits him in G.

That is enough on this subject. If anyone thinks that I have not discussed it sufficiently, he should practice everything I have

---

30. [D]ando di croce.

31. Agrippa is somewhat ambiguous here: *mandandola verso la parte diritta sua.*

demonstrated with the sword alone and the sword and dagger, and he will see that I have said as much as I needed to.

Chapter 17

The techniques with two swords, seen above, begin this way. The two opponents go on guard in C, and one of them goes from C to D, returns to C, goes to H, and returns again to D in order to confuse his opponent so that he does not know which attack is coming. Stepping forward with his left foot after making a feint to his enemy's eyes, he will engage in A, sending his adversary's weapon to his right side, and opposing[32] the right-hand sword, hit him in the chest in H. He should keep his left-hand sword free as he traverses, so that he can parry the enemy's weapons, and he should do all of this in one time. If the enemy does not save himself by jumping backward, I believe it would not be a bad thing for him to defend his chest by parrying by cover and then turn a *riverso* to the leg or a *stramazzone* to the head, since deceiving the attempt to engage[33] would not turn out well because his enemy's weapons get in the way.[34]

Now if the man on guard in C who was attacked above is instead on guard in F, then in the same time that the adversary, who is also on guard in C, makes the feint with his left foot forward, the man in F can launch an attack against the feint by turning away in G and hitting him either high in G or low in P, depending on where the enemy's feint is. If it is high, go low; if low, then go high. If it should seem to him that his thrust would fall short, he should wait fearlessly until after the man in C makes the feint and then beat the swords in A and, in the same time, flatten his body,

---

32. [S]*forzando.*
33. [S]*falsare de l'arme.*
34. In other words, the feints should be followed by cuts, for it will be difficult to return for a thrust because of the entanglement with the enemy's weapons.

Fig. 49. Case of Swords.

deceive the enemy's sword by disengaging above the blade,[35] and push forcefully between the enemy's weapons in G.

Looking at another case, suppose one adversary is on guard in D and the other is on guard in C. The man on guard in D can lower the point of his right-hand sword to the ground and then raise the enemy's sword with his false edge, pushing it to the adversary's left side. He should do this all in one time: supporting the right-hand sword by placing the left-hand one beneath it, he steps forward with his left foot, raises the adversary's sword, and stepping forward with his right foot, hits him with a low thrust. He can do this to either the right or the left side. The man in C can defend himself by bending at the waist and hit the enemy by pushing the latter's sword to the outside by opposing it with his left-hand sword. However, it would be better yet if he were to keep both of his swords still, so that when the enemy takes the step forward with his left foot in order to raise the swords, he can

---

35. *Standoli in prospettiva piana sflasar' la sua spada disopra.*

quickly move his right-hand sword backward and then hit him with it with a low thrust in countertime.

If the man on guard in C wants to attack the man on guard in D first, he can engage the latter's sword on the inside with his right sword, step forward with his left foot up against his right, and pressing the point down, follow by stepping forward with his right foot, turning his hand with the false edge, step forward with the left foot, and hit the adversary with the left-hand sword with a change of pressure.[36] However, he will be safer from the possibility of the enemy disengaging[37] if, instead of hitting with his left-hand sword, he presses down on the enemy's weapons and comes in close to hit him in the position of H. In order to defend against this, the fencer on guard in D can make a disengagement in time when the fencer on guard in C goes to engage and hit him (if only lightly on the hand or arm when he goes to engage the blade, which is why this is used only occasionally). If the enemy tries to hit in H, he can step back in B with his right hand held to the rear so that the middle of his sword is to the right of his head. Because the enemy takes such a big step forward, this will allow him to better void his *vita*, to beat away the blow with the left-hand sword, and to follow up by hitting the enemy in H.

Looking at another example, if one adversary is on guard in C and the other is in A and the latter wants to attack the former, he should quickly go into the position of D and, raising his left arm over his head, make a feint in the position F at his adversary's chest so that the latter uncovers his body. Then he can quickly beat aside the sword to hit him in the chest, withdraw his hand in the position of B so that the middle of the sword is to the right of his head, and lowering his left hand to make a better beat, attack the man on guard in A with a thrust in H or else withdraw his hand behind his knee so that the middle of the sword is to the right of the knee. From there, he can hit him in the chest in D on the outside over the sword. The fencer on guard in A, fearing

---

36. *Scambio di presa* — that is, the opposition of the blades.
37. *Sflasar' de l'arme.*

that the enemy will beat his sword aside and continue on to hit him, can defend himself by making a half-feint and then go to hit him on the outside in H as in the double figure above.[38] The same thing that goes for A goes for B, so I will not discuss it any further.

I could discuss many other techniques that you can do with two swords using guards other than those above, however it seems to me that I have shown enough with these examples and their explanations, and that by understanding the principles explained throughout the work for the single sword, sword and dagger, and sword and cape, you can do everything else you might need to do, such as feinting a *mandritto* and flinging a thrust on the traverse with your left-hand sword[39]; feinting with your left-hand sword and thrusting on the traverse with your right-hand sword; feinting a *mandritto*, parrying, beating with the left-hand sword, and cutting a *riverso*; feinting with the left-hand sword, beating, parrying with the right-hand sword, and cutting a *riverso*, etc. I, therefore, leave this to each reader to discover for himself by means of the examples and the various actions described here.

Chapter 18

The application of this grappling technique begins this way. Suppose a fencer on guard in C engages[40] a fencer on guard in B on the outside and follows by attacking in H by opposition up to the part where he turns his chest then recovers in the position of B and thrusts again by opposition in the position of H, and suppose that the adversary, also going into the position of H, parries on the outside to turn a *stramazzone*. The first fencer, who was on guard in C but who is now in B, can go into the position of H and turn his hand to parry by crossing the enemy's blade in front and, stepping forward with his left foot, seize the enemy's arm as seen in the figure denoted by S and Q.

---

38. See pp. 80–81.
39. *Ferir di mano manca lanciata.*
40. *Tastare,* literally "to taste" or "to feel out."

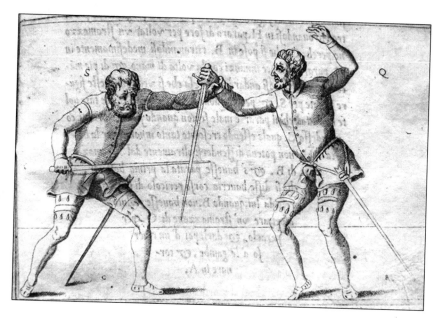

Fig. 50. Grappling, S vs. Q.

This is the logical thing to do because of what I have said many times: it is bad to parry if you are not forced to. Thrusting in H made the fencer who was on guard in C come so far forward that he could not have otherwise defended himself from a *stramazzone* from the fencer on guard in B, and after parrying the latter's cut it would have been dangerous for him remain so close to him, since B would not have waited to parry C's *stramazzone* and then give him a *riverso* to the leg and step back in A.

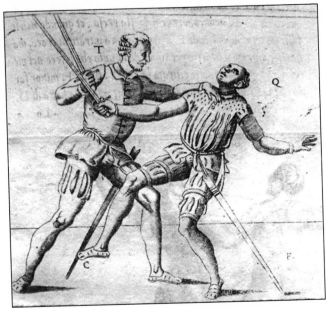

Fig. 51. Grappling, T vs. Q.

CHAPTER 19

Here the stronger man, Q, is shown being thrown by the weaker man, T. If the weaker man goes on guard in C and the stronger in F, and the former advances in the position of F to engage the enemy's sword on the inside, and the enemy thrusts to his chest by opposition, then the man who was on guard in C (who went into F), can yield to the force by lowering his sword with a back-handed movement,[41] and in one time, step forward with his right foot and turn his right hand. Stepping across with his left foot in the same time, he can place his left hand on the enemy's collar and make this throw.

---

41. *Abassando la spada à riverso per cedere à la forza.*

If you can't do this because the stronger man, who is in F, does not attack by opposition but rather retracts his arm out of fear of the feint,[42] then in the same time he retracts his sword, the weaker man, who is in F, can step across to the other's left side with a thrust in D.

CHAPTER 20

This grappling technique begins in this way: if a fencer on guard in C uses a big action to attack someone on guard in D with a *mandritto* to the head, and the latter replies by parrying in A and cutting a *mandritto* to the head, the former can parry in front with a high cover, traverse forward with his left leg, and turn his left arm under his enemy's right arm. This is seen above, where the letter V is placed by the victor and the letter Q by the vanquished.

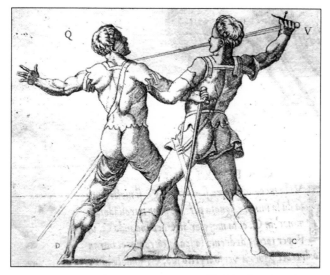

Fig. 52. Grappling, Q vs. V.

---

42. That is, the pressure of the engagement in F, which Agrippa considers as a feint.

This sort of thing happens to inexperienced people, because if the fencer on guard in D had stopped his cut in midair when he was turning the *mandritto* to the head of the fencer on guard in C, turned the point, and thrust in H, he would have been able to hit the enemy in the chest, or by stepping in with his left foot, use the throw shown by S and Q.

CHAPTER 21

If a fencer on guard in O wants to hit someone on guard in C, he can make him move by feinting to his face while stepping forward with his left foot next to his right, lowering his point, and when the enemy makes a *mandritta*, taking a counter-step to give him a low thrust in the position of C while guarding his head with his shield.[43] If however, the man on guard in C is experienced and does not move his shield to react to the feint, then in that time the first fencer can thrust to his adversary's right shoulder and recover in the position of O with a *riverso*.

From there, you can use the throw shown below by the fencers marked T and Q in two ways. In the first, you step with your right foot close to your left and feint a *mandritto* when the adversary moves his leg.[44] When he goes to parry it, give him a *riverso* to the leg, and then, all in the same time, turn the sword to the inside with the right edge outward,[45] follow[46] with the right foot, step with the left, and so take hold of him for the throw.

If you can't turn your sword to the inside because his leg is too close or the sword is too heavy, the other method is to lower the hilt of your sword while keeping the point up, close in[47] with your right foot, and follow with your left foot.

---

43. *Trapassando à mandritta del nemico.*
44. Or "changes his stance"—*a la volta de le gambe de l'aversario.*
45. Again, similar to saber prime.
46. *Stringeria.*
47. *Stringendo.*

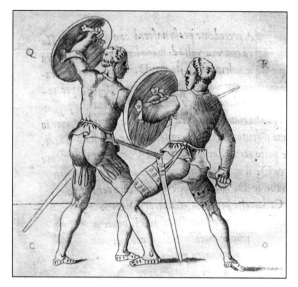

Fig. 53. Sword and Shield, Q vs. T.

If you don't want to make the throw, rather than finishing the feint with the edge, turn your hand from low to high, cover your right knee with your shield to defend against the adversary's *riverso*, and finish the attack with a thrust.[48]

Chapter 22

As I have discussed and demonstrated with these techniques, parrying with all the offensive and defensive weapons I have discussed is almost always detrimental. I will now show how this is so with the

---

48. *Stringendo di punta.* Agrippa uses the verb *stringere* ["to bind, to wrinch, to guird in, to claspe, to clinch," according to Florio] in three different ways in this passage. Jared Kirby in his 2004 translation of Capo Ferro defines *stringere* as "making a firm but supple contact on the adversary's weapon." Tommaso Leoni, in his 2005 translation of Fabris, defines it as a synonym for "finding the sword" *(trovare la spada)*, that is, positioning your weapon with mechanical advantage.

Fig. 54. Sword and Shield, Q vs. P.

shield. In the same time that the man in the position of O feints a low *mandritto*, the fencer on guard in C, not parrying but rather feigning to parry, can go and hit the former in countertime with a thrust in P, as shown in the following example — or indeed in any attack made with a feint.

CHAPTER 23

This example shows the same thing. Suppose fencer C goes into the position of E to attack his adversary with a thrust in D. The opponent is also in the position of E, holding his shield open so that he invites the attack. At the same time as fencer C goes into E to make the thrust in D, the man on guard in E does not do anything to defend except void his *vita* and counter-step to his enemy's left side and make a thrust to his flank in the position of P, as is seen here.

Also, suppose one of them is perhaps in E and the other in D, and that the fencer on guard in D craftily comes in with the point of his sword close to the ground, holding his shield open so as to expose his chest. As soon as the man on guard in E goes to thrust in D, then all in one time the adversary meets the thrust in the position of F, changes to parry with the shield, and makes a thrust or a *riverso* in P while raising his shield over his head, turn-

Fig. 55. Sword and Shield, D vs. P.

ing his *vita*[49] and counter-stepping to the enemy's left side if he has to, as seen here.

Many different attacks can be made from these two guards, and each one can counter the other — that is a feint with the point, a parry with the shield, and a high *riverso*; a low *mandritto*, a parry with the shield, and a *riverso* to the leg; a high *mandritto*, a parry with the shield, and a *riverso* to the head; a feint to the outside and a *riverso*

---

49.   That is, turning at the waist.

to the right leg; feinting a cut to the head and cutting to the leg; a feint to the leg and a *mandritto* to the head; a low *mandritto*, a parry with the shield, and a feint or a *riverso* with the left foot against the right, finishing with a thrust in G and a step backward with the right foot while cutting a *riverso*; a low feint, a high attack, and return to the rear with a *riverso*; a high feint, a low hit, and a return to the rear with a *riverso* while parrying with the shield; finding the opposing sword, raising it with the false edge, making a round *mandritto* to the leg, and returning to the rear. You can do these with all sorts of weapons. Many other attacks are possible as well, which I will refrain from discussing so as not to fatigue the reader. You can judge for yourself how to defend against them — and also how not to — using the reasoning I have given.

CHAPTER 24

While your longing for victory may be such that you are moved to take up a vendetta for some trivial cause, this seems to me to

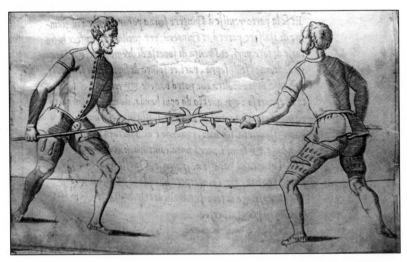

Fig. 56. Staff Weapons.

be all pomp and vain exhibitionism, for to so conduct oneself with weapons will be to the detriment of he who so uses them. Therefore, finishing the part in which we have discussed the principles of the use of arms, we turned to the application, which we have discussed up until this point. We are now therefore at the place where we discuss hafted weapons.

If you make a feint to the enemy's outside, that is his left side, then as soon as he goes to parry, disengage in time and thrust to the other side. If you feint to the inside, disengage the enemy's weapon and thrust to the outside. If high, disengage and hit him low. If low, evade and hit him high.

If he thrusts to the other side without parrying while you are making the evasion, parry and thrust in whatever way you made the feint. If on the outside, parry and thrust on the outside; if on the inside, parry and thrust on the inside; if above, parry and thrust above; if below, parry and thrust below. Also, you can beat and make the thrust with a traverse to any side, holding the haft[50] of the weapon in such a way that you can thrust with it. If your adversary does not thrust, then you should still feint, counter-step, and thrust.

And if the enemy neither parries nor thrusts, then the moment after the feint, you should feint, beat, and thrust. Therefore following the feint, feint on the outside, beat, and thrust on the outside; or feint on the inside, beat, and thrust on the inside, and so on.

And if you find yourself as seen above [fig. 58],[51] everyone should understand that a stronger man does not have the advantage and, in fact, helps the man of lesser strength by pushing. Giving a moment of resistance, he can invite the enemy to push as strongly as he can, and in the same time that he obliges, unlock the weapons with a pull to the right, and sending the enemy's force to the outside, hit him while escaping unharmed.

---

50. Agrippa's word is *calce*, which (according to Florio) also refers to the place by which one holds a tilting lance.

51. The engraving shows the heads of the halberds locked. Di Grassi gives a different answer for this dilemma, advising the fencer to raise the adversary's weapon and stab him in the chest with the butt-spike.

If perhaps you both lock your hooks and pull, the weaker man should move his right foot close to his left, turning his waist[52] so that the adversary sees him in profile, giving way and pushing towards him at the moment to unlock the hooks, and then, swiveling his waist quickly back, send the enemy's weapon to the outside. Regaining your hold on the weapon, hit him by stepping forward with your left foot. And if the stronger man neither pushes nor gives way, but rather pulls toward himself, at the same time the weaker man steps forward with his left foot, thrusting as I just described.

CHAPTER 25

I had also planned to say something about how to use the two-handed sword. However, anything I say will be useless because of the

uncertain rules that govern its blows, which travel so through the air.[53] It seems sufficient for me to say that anyone who does not know how to use it, but who wishes to, should not try reasoning it out, since any advice or ordering will only confuse you without proper lessons and demonstrations from someone of this profession. I only advise that two people fighting with two-handed swords can make the same thrusts described above with hafted weapons.

Fig. 57. The Two-Handed Sword.

---

52. *Vita.*
53. That is, the principles of *tacto, forza* and leverage do not apply.

Fig. 58. Mounted Combat.

CHAPTER 26[54]

Now we come to the equestrian section. After sufficiently discussing combat on foot, it ought to be easy to speak of fighting on horseback. However, I cannot give certain rules for any science. I have not sufficiently studied the art since, due to the ever-increasing inconvenience, I have not been able to practice fighting on horseback. Still, speaking from the example of combat on foot, I should be naturally able to say something useful and profitable about the same thing on horseback. I do not, however, wish to do so. Since I am not free to say everything about this practice, or at least about the greater part, I do not want to entangle myself with it. Therefore, I will leave this task to those who can more easily practice this art and, placing this at the end of my discussion of combat on foot, I will say nothing more.

---

54. This is misnumbered "XXII" in the original.

Fig. 59. Agrippa's Dream.

DIALOGUE OF CAMILLO AGRIPPA AND ANNIBALE CARO

I pondered for many days whether I ought to publish, in addition to the discourse on arms, a certain conversation that Annibale Caro and I had over the course of three days. This took place because of a certain vision I had, which I will discuss later. Finally, leaning more towards the affirmative than the negative, motivated by my own arguments, and also encouraged by my friend, I allowed myself to be persuaded and permitted it to be printed.

I therefore ask everyone who might read it — whether by chance, or because of some whim, or for some other reason — to pay attention to the reasons that I had it published. Although I claim it as my own work, I excuse myself on the grounds that one cannot easily resist one's friends, since such a thing would not be very praiseworthy, and also that I do not wish to be numbered among the learned, but rather open to discussing all matters. This small ordering of words remains a friend to everyone equally, and equally commended to everyone.[1]

---

1. The dialogue takes place at Annibale's house; he is plainly one of Agrippa's patrons, and, in a tradition as old as Rome, it is Agrippa's role as client to attend Annibale at his home. Despite this, in the dialogue their courtly speech indicates they wish to be portrayed as of equal rank (despite Annibale's sometimes playing the fool for the purpose of pedagogy).

Annibale and Camillo

Annibale. Welcome!

Camillo. It's good to see you, my friend. How can I help you?

A. *I* don't want anything — it's on your account that I wished to see *you*.

C. And I, for my account, have come to visit you, so it's all for the best. But why are you upset?

A. I'm not upset, God protect me. I don't want to give you bad news, but rather to warn you about something.

C. Of what?

A. That you don't try to print your book — as I understand you have set out to do — until you explain the meaning of the geometrical figures that you've placed in three or four places — if I remember correctly — since they can confuse the readers and might be understood otherwise than you intended.

C. Thanks for the warning, and you're just in time since I was just coming for your permission to do exactly that. I had thought that the brief explanation I had already written was enough, but your understanding is much greater than mine — and I fully agree with it because last night, I had a vision of being attacked by certain philosophers. They were completely against my making with the stick those figures that you mentioned, or talking about certain other things that I have discussed with you, Alessandro Corvino, and Francesco Siciliano many times. Rather, they thought me presumptuous for wanting to discuss such matters without having studied them. After that, it seemed to me that I defended myself with the help of many gentlemen who were friends of mine.

I wasn't going to say anything else about it, but if some students of Euclid or of Aristotle want to drag my name through the mud, I will defend myself as best I can, both on my own and with the help of my patrons.[2] So I'm quite eager to explain the diagram to correct any false interpretations and also to show to the world that, truly, if I have not studied a subject, I can still naturally speak reasonably on it. If you want to see the proof for yourself, take my book in hand and find the diagram, so that I can show you by the letters how it's done — that is, if you think that it's worth the effort.

A.   Of course, it certainly seems worthwhile, because it seems to me truly to be a wonderful work. Also, maybe you can use what you've already written on the subject. Here's the book and here's the figure you spoke of.

C.   So, first to make a circle, you place one point of the stick on a plane, like so, and turn it with your other hand so that it comes back to where it began.[3]

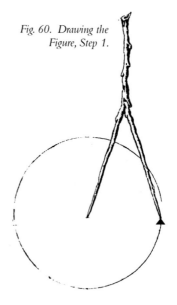

Fig. 60. Drawing the Figure, Step 1.

---

2.   Perhaps an oblique reference to the Bolognese Dardi school of fencing, whose founder was also a professor of mathematics at the university. Certainly, the principles of Agrippa's fencing, as well as his cosmogony, are derived from Euclid and Aristotle.

3.   In other words, the fork of the stick is used like a compass.

This is how to make the circle. From here, beginning with the point on the circumference marked A, as you can see, you make a hexagram by walking it around inside the circle, returning to the starting point like so. I can, by moving the instrument by two intervals of the hexagon, draw a line from A to B, then, skipping another two spaces finish at C, and thus, as you can see, make a triangle.

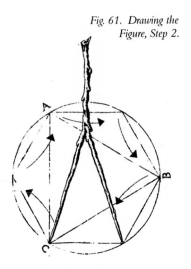

Fig. 61. Drawing the Figure, Step 2.

A. Are both the triangle and the hexagon within the circumference of the circle?

C. Yes, both of them are. If you want to make a square, divide the circle by the diameter with two points marked by the letters D and E.[4] Put one point of the piece of wood on D, rotate the other, and note where it intersects the circumference of the circle.[5] Do the same thing on point E. Then, do the same thing at the points of intersection, and where the two semi-circles form an X is point F. From point F, draw a long line downward through the center of the circle toward point G. By drawing lines from one point to another, you will make a perfect square within the circumference of the circle.[6]

---

4. It is important that D be on one of the vertices of the hexagon.

5. Agrippa specifically says to put the divider on point D, though it would be easier to merely put it on one of the points of the hexagon (see the diagram).

6. That is, drawing lines from point D to the points where the line from F to G intersects the circumference of the circle to point E to point G will form the square.

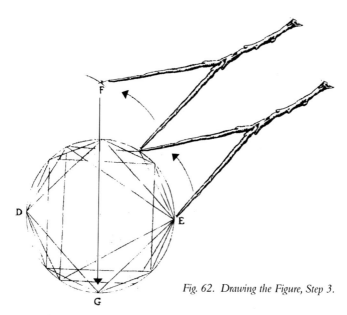

Fig. 62. Drawing the Figure, Step 3.

A. What else can you show me from what you've demonstrated here, and how do you do it?

C. If you want to do the same thing that you just did one more time, put one point of the stick on D and turn it. Do the same with G and again find where the semicircles cross midway between them. Do the same thing between points E and F and the other two corners of the square. By drawing diameters from these points through the middle of the circle and connecting the points where they intersect with the circumference of the circle, you will make a second square the same size as the other.

A. And how is the octagon made inside the circle?

C. Here's how to make the octagon: connect the corners of the squares, just as you did the first time, and you'll make the octagon without having to draw any other lines, since as you saw, the first square generated the second from itself. If you want to make another octagon with lines the same size as the length of the forked part of the stick — that is, the diameter of the circle — follow this rule. First, find the corners of the small squares, which are in the middle of the sides of the bigger, as you can see, and then connect them. In this way, you make two squares inside the circle. Put the compass on the corners of the small squares, draw the semicircles, and by connecting the places where they intersect outside the circle, you will form the large octagon.

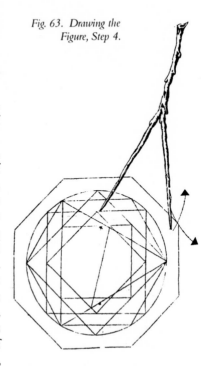

Fig. 63. Drawing the Figure, Step 4.

A. You say that in order to make the smaller squares from which you draw the octagon, you have to connect points in the middle of the sides of the larger squares. How do you know where the midpoints of the lines are?

C. Easy. I didn't say how to do it at first since I thought everyone would be able to discover the method for themselves, but here it is: you draw lines from the vertices of the angles of the first octagon through its diameter and so find the vertices of the smaller squares. These are, as I have said, in the middle of the sides of the larger.

A. How can you use the stick to make a pentagon from this last figure?

C. You use it, but not to measure with. Rather, you measure with this small line, which comes from the two small squares and the triangle. Coming from here, it intersects them, passing through the middle of the circle, close to the center. By moving this around the circumference, you form the pentagon.[7]

A. And the oval, too?

C. Also the oval, as well as many other different figures. However, since this is not my vocation, I don't want to waste any more time in it. I would very much like to show you how to make a sphere from an octagon, but I can explain how to do it another time, since it's getting late and I would like to go and write down the little discussion we just had and use it for the purpose that you suggested to me.

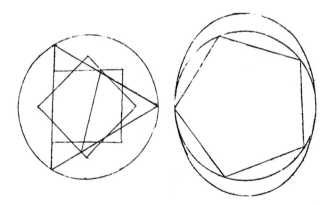

Fig. 64. Drawing the Figure, Step 5.

---

7. Agrippa is somewhat obscure here, perhaps to challenge the reader. The line shown in the diagram is the exact length of the sides of the pentagon, and can merely be walked around the circumference to make the pentagon. The line is formed by placing the stick/compass on two points where the squares intersect and rotating them until they intersect with the triangle and then connecting the two points. The pentagon is, of course, the inside of a pentagram (a figure of great significance to Vitruvius, Henry Cornelius Agrippa, and Horapollo).

A. I agree that it's best to do that while your memory is fresh. But do not go to the printer's until you have everything in order, and perhaps tomorrow I can learn about the octagon and the sphere. In any case it won't be printed tomorrow, since it's a holiday. Still, you seem to have everything in order, and so if I can perhaps prevail upon you to talk about it some more tomorrow, I will await you.

C. That's a good plan. I will come tomorrow, so good evening!

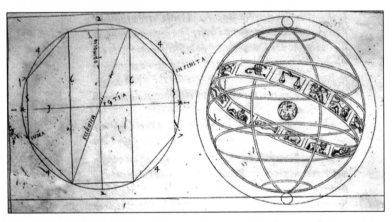

Fig. 65. The Heavenly Sphere and Its Geometrical Representation.

C. God save you!

A. Welcome!

C. Yesterday I came for one reason, and the opposite happened to me. Today I come to discuss the widest possible implications of what I promised to discuss with you, and I don't know what will happen.

A. That pleases me, but meanwhile, please won't you perhaps tell me whether something troubled you on your way home?

C. Nothing troubled me, but I didn't hear from you what I wanted to hear about turning over my book to the printer. I would like it very much if you gave me permission to do so today.

A. Certainly we'll do that, but first, explain how to make a sphere from an octagon as you promised you would.

C. Indeed, I said yesterday that I would show you how to form a sphere from an octagon. Look, I'll show you how. First note on this diagram that I have marked with the number 1 what are, according to conventional wisdom, the two fixed poles. I have marked the circle of the equator with a 2, the meridian with a 3, the *colure* with a 4;[8] the frigid zone with a 5, the temperate with a 6, the two imaginary poles with a 7, and the zodiac — or the ecliptic, as we also might call it — with an 8. And this forms a sphere, as you can see in the figure I have right here.[9]

A. This pleases me greatly. Truthfully, what you have just told me is a good discovery. But tell me, since we are discussing the sphere, what might you have done differently? Haven't you spoken according to conventional wisdom? Do you believe otherwise?

---

8. *Coluro,* "great circles imagined in heaven meeting in the poles of the world, of which there are two principal," according to Florio. The meridians of the celestial sphere.

9. Rotate the diagram ninety degrees counter-clockwise to place it in its proper orientation.

C. I do not know if I believe otherwise, but my opinion concerning the poles is that they aren't points that hold up the machinery of the cosmos. Rather, it is closer to the truth that the swift motion of the spheres, which were set in motion[10] by the Infinite Power, revolves around axes on either end of the circumference, which we call poles, rather than the poles holding it up as do those on which a physical sphere turns.

A. What does it rest on, then, if you don't think it's the poles?

C. It appears to me to be something else besides the poles. It is supported on this thing, which does not come from the first motion, but is united together with it, and which can not logically be called a pole.

A. What is the thing that holds it up, then, if you don't think it's the poles?

C. It is the center of the space, which is the cause of the motion.

A. The center of what space?

C. The intersection of the meridian line with the equator, which divides the axis in half.

A. How can you say this motion comes from the center, since you said a moment ago the whole machinery was created first? Perhaps this center came first, or perhaps the power was created by it? [11]

C. Not *from* it, but *through* it, and it was created in such a way that all created things must come from it. The spheres, because of their concavity and their having been created so perfect in themselves, cannot descend to the center. Nor can they be placed over the earth because of the space between it and

---

10. Agrippa says *imaginata*—imagined by God, who created the world with a thought.

11. Annibale's objection is informed by Aristotelian physics, which holds that the created thing is inferior to the creator, and thus can not set the creator in motion.

them. Rather, because they unceasingly turn around without resting, they are the cause of the motion.

A. I accept this as true insofar as the poles and the cause of the motion go, but I also want to know if it is this inward motion that makes the two lines that you spoke of. Do they join the spheres to the center as the equinox does?

C. That's a good question and a difficult one for me to respond to. I don't know how to answer it save with an argument that I will demonstrate presently, and which I am confident will satisfy you.[12]

A. Thank you for that. Now tell me how one might perhaps arrive at your conclusions by a different route.

C. Now, whether for good or ill, we come to the meat of the argument. To me it appears that in this machine's creation,[13] by turning through the warm zone, it scattered the seven planets. As I have said, although they are attracted to the center, they cannot descend because of the concavity of their spheres. They relate to the eighth sphere itself, and travel on the route they have taken around the equator because of their mass,[14] avoiding the lighter regions like the four temperate and the frigid zones — and I say "lighter" with respect to the spheres.

A. Then the planets must have mass.

C. And who doubts it? If the planets did not have mass, wouldn't all the spheres travel in the same manner? Certainly they would

---

12. Literally, *nondimeno ancora che l'anima non mi porga di saper' lalagar' sopra cio ragione alcuna, eccetto versimile, tuttavia ne parlelo per quanto comporta quel poco giudico che mi diede natura, piu presto in vero per satisfare a voi che per cosa ch' io confidi dover' dire che bona sia* ("the spirit has not moved me to know how to answer that argument in any way, except similarly, still speaking with the faculty of the small amount of judgment that nature gave me, in truth I will soon satisfy you with a thing that I am confident will be good"). Agrippa never uses one word when twenty will suffice!

13. I.e., the cosmos.

14. Agrippa says *gravezza*, "heaviness," which I have translated as the marginally more scientifically accurate *mass*.

turn on a single pole, but because they move or rest according to two unmoving points on a circumference that moves or rests in various ways, one ought to believe they have mass.

A. And since they are heavy, their mass is enough to bend the motion of the last sphere along the route of the equator, since they cannot stay on a fixed pole?

C. As I argued above, because they revolve and are scattered outside the line of the equator, with each one pressing on the center, they have to follow the first motion or otherwise they would stop on the poles.

A. That is, those of Saturn.

C. And of the others also.

A. Why the others? Do not the two created poles serve them all?

C. It seems to me they cannot, and the reason is that they all do not rest on the ecliptic, as Saturn does, but rather all differently, after the first positions they were placed in by the Highest Power. As manifest experience shows us — and one ought to agree with what everyone has affirmed — each has fixed its poles differently from the others, and from this come the greater and lesser lengths of the zodiac.

A. How much smaller and larger? Do you find it to be more or less than 12 degrees?

C. As I have said, according to my reasoning it can be 12 degrees and less than 11, and more than 13, 14, and 15. Because they are contained by their poles, and they lengthen or restrict their rotation thereby, one cannot say that it is only 12 degrees, or deny that it is sometimes 11 or 13, 14 or 15.

A. Can you tell me why these planets don't space themselves out equally?

C. And I'll give you certain proof.

A. What does that mean? Certain or uncertain, say what it means!

C.   I think there are two possible causes. The one is that a planet
can move very far away or very close according to its violent
motion[15]; the other, that the one weighs more or less than the
others.

A.   And for this reason you conclude that the sun goes outside
the ecliptic. Is it not true?

C.   As to the center of the sun, there is no doubt; as to all its
body, I cannot agree. Reasoning entirely from appearances, it
seems to me that that if in the end perhaps I agree with one
conclusion, other people, following different reasoning, will
agree with the other conclusions.

A.   Right now I do not wish to be someone else. Rather, so as not
to stand in the way of the truth, I will agree with whatever
you say it is. Therefore, tell me how your rules explain the
different motions of the moon, which is now up and now
down, now here and now there, now closer and now further
away.

C.   Perhaps that is so, and here's why. The moon does not move
under its own power, but at the same time, it cannot stand
still, because the highest sphere, with the aid of the others,
lifts it up — relative to us — and carries it here and there, in
and out, according to the turning of its poles. Do you think
it would travel in this fashion if it could make the different
movements that you suggested?

A.   Why do you say relative to us?

C.   Because to us it seems that it moves on its own and revolves
relative to us, who stand on the surface of the earth. Relative
to the center of the universe though, it only moves forward
and backward.

A.   Isn't the center of the universe the same as that of the
earth?

15.   That is, Aristotle's idea of "violent motion," which goes against the
"natural" movement — downward, with gravity, toward the center of the
universe — because of some force.

C.   No, *signore!* The center of the universe and the center of the world are not the same. You will see the proof of this another time, for now is the time to go, since the afternoon heat is beginning to bother me. I will come to visit another time and more comfortably explain to you what I mean.

A.   This plan to come again pleases me, but in order that giving me an answer does not inconvenience you, I won't keep you as late as today. I will see you tomorrow, but a little earlier than today because I have decided to review the business with the press a little.

C.   Honestly, I did not remember the press and didn't think to return, for God knows when it would have occurred to me to pay such close attention to this subject. But now let's continue, and I'll kill two birds with one stone.[16] May God go with you.

A.   Adieu.

\ʚɞ/

C.   Here I am! God save you, I have come.

A.   Welcome. Can we get to work now? Have a seat. Good! What shall we do? Where are these two centers?

C.   Hold on, let me sit a moment before you order me around! The one is the center of the cosmos, the other the center of the earth. Didn't we say that yesterday?

A.   Yes, because the earth isn't in the universe.

C.   Slow down! What I'm trying to say is that the universe has one center in itself, and the earth another.

A.   It's the same thing.

C.   Actually, no, it's not — that of the universe is the one around which the spheres rotate, and that of the earth is in the center of its circumference.[17]

---

16. Agrippa literally says, "I'll accomplish two tasks with one trip" (*farò un viaggio, & doi servitii*).

17. That is, the center of the universe (Agrippa uses *mondo*, which translates literally to "world," but here refers to the Ptolemaic universe) is the point around

A. How can that be true? The earth is in the center of the universe, and the center of the world is the center, so isn't it true that the center of the universe, around which the spheres rotate, is also the center of the earth?

C. It would be if the earth were always the same weight.

A. What? Does it get lighter with each rotation?

C. Not all of it, except in one part.

A. What are you trying to say?

C. That the intrinsic qualities of the cosmos make it that way.

A. How?

C. By putting the heavy and weighty humors in one part of the earth and then pushing them to the other side, which then becomes heavier by however much lighter it becomes where it is hot.

A. How can the lighter part rise again in such a system?

C. It will always become heavy again in the same way that it was made lighter.

A. Then the earth must be mobile.

C. If my reasoning is correct, it cannot be otherwise. Because of the way the universe is constructed, the center, against which the weight of the earth rests, could not allow it to be any other way.

A. If it is as you say, and your reasoning is correct, can you prove it?

C. I believe I can. If you were to mark a star in on the horizontal below the arctic in the winter, in January or February, and another above it at the same distance from the horizontal, and then try to find them again in the summer, in July or August, you will see that they have moved.

A. Why does the star appear in the winter but not in the summer?

---

which the heavenly spheres rotate, while the earth's center is in the middle of its diameter. Rotation around a center is Aristotle's seventh type of motion.

C. One changes places with the other — that is, the one marked above on the artic will take the place of the one on the horizontal, and the one on the horizontal will take the place of the one on the artic.

A. Can you demonstrate this with another proof?

C. In the summer the star marked by the horizontal disappears in the same way the star marked in the winter does. And similarly, if you want to prove it in the winter with the star marked in the summer, it will make the proof another way.

A. Why does this happen?

C. It ascends higher in the sky, which comes to cover the star on the horizontal.

A. Is there anything this proof does not explain?

C. This phenomenon can be explained in other ways, but they do not explain why this happens.

A. And if someone says this is not a good explanation?

C. As soon as he observes great and natural things with the necessary diligence, he will see the truth of it.

A. And if one does not wish to believe it?

C. If, according to your supposition, certain people do not yet wish to believe it, I can show them the course of the sun, that of the moon, its waxing and waning, the opposition between them, the interposition of the earth between them, the quantity of the zodiac, and other secrets of the heavens on a physical sphere,[18] as I have done before you, Alessandro Ruffino, Iacomo del Negro, Hieronimo Garimberto, Francesco Salviati, and Alessandro Greco, as well as an infinite number of other virtuous and honored men.

A. I remember, and you were a wonderful teacher. You can claim it to your credit to be the discoverer of such a thing in our times.

---

18. I.e., an astrological armature.

C. I believe I have, perhaps presumptuously, already done so — as you are no doubt aware, I had already planned to do so in the beginning of the Treatise on Arms.

A. Truly, you have performed wonderfully. But what will you do about this work of yours?

C. What would you advise me to do?

A. Nothing other than what I have already said to you, except that you should add the explanation of the geometrical figures and happily turn it over to the press.

C. And I will do so. Good evening, Adieu!

APPENDIX

AGRIPPA'S WEAPON

In considering Italian edged weapons of the sixteenth century, one can notice a general trend for the weapons to become longer, with the blades tapering at the *debole* (the "weak" part of the blade, nearest the point) to balance them more for thrusting (though they still maintained a very dangerous cutting ability), and the hilts growing to encircle the unarmed sword-hand in a protective cage of steel. Whether this is a cause or an effect of Agrippa's work can, of course, be debated. Nonetheless, the fact remains that during his lifetime, the Milanese engineer witnessed a gradual change in preference from medieval-style cutting and thrusting swords to "modern" thrusting weapons designed to be used according to the principles elucidated in his *Trattato*.

Montaigne recalls, on his famous 1580–81 trip to Italy, having dinner in Florence with a very conservative professional soldier named Silvio Piccolomini who — in addition to hating artillery — was very critical of the new way of fencing, maintaining that holding the sword in front made it easy for the enemy to dominate the blade, and that the custom of first making the thrust, then making another attack, and then stopping was quite against what people actually do in fighting.[1] Likewise, Camillo Palladini, in his manuscript composed circa 1560, and Girolamo Lucino, in his 1589 printed work, mention Agrippa by name and contrast their own methods with his.[2]

---

1.   Michel de Montaigne, *Journal de Voyage de Michel de Montaigne en Italie par la Suisse et l'Allemagne en 1580 et 1581* (Rome, 1774), 1: 134. For an English version, see *The Journal of Montaigne's Travels in Italy,* trans. by W.G. Waters (London: J. Murray, 1903), p. 103. My thanks to Matt Galas for this reference.

2.   On Palladini, see William Gaugler, *The History of Fencing* (Bangor, Maine: Laureate Press, 1998), 10–15; on Lucino, see Giovanni Romani, *Storia di Casalmaggiore* (Casalmaggiore: Fratelli Bizzarri, 1830), 10: 326. My

In order to evaluate the sorts of swords use by Agrippa's audience, I recorded statistics and notes from a selection of contemporary weapons in the collection of the Metropolitan Museum of Art. The difficulty of such a study is twofold. First, one cannot ascertain the true "feel" of a weapon from statistics alone — though such details as weight and balance can give us an idea of general trends. The second is that relatively few complete weapons survive from this time period. Not only were many weapons modified or re-hilted either within the sword's working life or in the centuries thereafter, but there was a veritable industry in the nineteenth and early twentieth centuries cobbling together the parts of disparate weapons, and even fabricating entirely new ones, for the benefit of the sort of wealthy enthusiasts whose collections formed the basis of the museum's holdings. Often, it can be difficult to discern an original from a complete fake. A curator's learned appraisal can help to differentiate sixteenth-century design from nineteenth, but another important — though admittedly biased — test is the overall feel of the weapon. Could this weapon have been used in a sensible manner — or is it perhaps simply a poor-quality original, since weapons then, as now, came in various grades of quality?

My observations have been noted in the table below. All measurements are in inches.

thanks to Matt Galas for bringing Lucino to light and Ilkka Hartikainen for the reference.

Accession Number	Date/ Provenance	Blade Length	Overall Length (Maximum)	Blade Width	Overall Width (Maximum)	Blade Thickness
1. 14.25.1106	c.1535–40 Italian?	44 1/4	49 3/4	1 5/16	4 1/4	1/4
2. 04.3.21 "'Rapier' of Charles V"	1546	36 5/8	42	1 5/16	6 1/2	5/16
3. 42.50.25	c.1550? Brescia	36 3/8	41 1/2	1 5/16	7 3/16	5/16
4. 04.3.24	c.1550–1660	40 1/2	47 1/4	1 3/8	NG	1/2
5.14.25.987	c.1550–60 Italian (per A.V.B. Norman)	37	43 1/4	1 1/2	NG	1/4

Hardness	Weight	Balance (from Bottom of Pommel)	Remarks
50–55	3 lbs 5 oz	9 1/2	Described on object card as perhaps French, c. 1500–1550, this was excavated in the Vendée and is similar to a sword in the Landes-Museum in Zurich. Somewhat heavy and perhaps left-handed, this is a cutting weapon despite its long blade.
60-70	2 lbs 11 oz	10 1/4	Blackened steel hilt damasked in gold and silver. Simple hilt with pas d'anes and two prongs *(parier-knebel)*. Identical to a sword in the Real Armeria in Madrid attributed to Charles V and decorated exactly like one in a portrait of Edward VI by Scrots, c. 1551–52, and an Italian armor, purchased from the Negroli in 1546, also at Madrid. Boccia, Coelho, and La Rocca (the first two on the object card, the third in a verbal opinion) opine that both swords were made by the Negroli as part of a garniture (for practical, not parade, use) in June and July of 1546. Normally on display in the glass case at the Met, this weapon has a diamond-cross section blade tapering to a strong point, and very much wants to cut. Despite its elaborate ornamentation (as befitting its purchaser), this is a good example of a typical working sword of the early sixteenth century, equally well suited to battlefield or civilian use.
55–65	2 lbs 10 oz	11 1/2	This weapon, which is usually on display in the case at the Met's Arms and Armor Gallery, possesses an extremely unusual blade with a "grid" pattern and a very acute point. A note by Boccia on the object card dates it to Lombardy, c. 1560–70. The hilt is blackened steel damascened in silver. Pas d'anes, two rings, knuckle guard, pear-shaped pommel. It is likely a composite, however, as the ricasso, which has gold arabesque instead of silver, has been ground down to fit the hilt, obliterating some of the pattern. Marked with the monogram of Prince Karl of Lichtenstein, in whose family's possession it once was. Awkwardly point heavy, but this evaluation is of dubious utility since it is a probable remount.
45–60	3 lbs 9/17 oz	13	Though not noted in the object card, this weapon is far too unwieldy to be entirely original.
60–75	2 lbs 6 oz	11 1/2	Flattened triangular pommel, broad, recurved quillions, parier-knebel on hilt. The blade, which fits exactly flush with the hilt, is engraved as having been made by Domingo "al maestro" (marked MAE ★ STRE ★); it has three fullers and an effective point of ogive shape. It is a wonderfully well-balanced cutting weapon. Norman opines that the hilt is Italian, c. 1550, as a similar weapon is illustrated in Filippo Orso's drawings of 1554. As per a

Accession Number	Date/ Provenance	Blade Length	Overall Length (Maximum)	Blade Width	Overall Width (Maximum)	Blade Thickness
5. 14.25.987 (cont.)						
6. 1972.269.9	c.1560 Italian	40 3/16	47	1 3/8	11	1/4
7. 1973.27.2	1560 Milan	27 1/8	34 1/2	1 13/16	NG	1/4
8. 14.25.1190	c.1570 Italy (per Boccia)	43 5/8	49 1/8	7/8	NG	3/16
9. 14.25.1155	c.1570 northern Italy or France (per Boccia)	35 5/8	41 1/8	1 1/4	NG	3/16
10. 04.3.287	c.1570 Spanish?	41 1/4	47 1/2	1 1/8	NG	1/4
11. 11.89.4	c.1580 Italian	40 1/8	46	15/16	8 1/4	3/16

Hardness	Weight	Balance (from Bottom of Pommel)	Remarks
			note on the object card, Phyrr believes that the blade might be of nineteenth-century manufacture (authentic markings were stamped, not engraved); however, according to another note on the object card, Boccia, based on the weapon's balance and feel, believes the blade to be genuine and the signature to be a later addition. Normally on display at the Met's Arms and Armor Gallery.
NG	2 lb 11 oz	12 3/4	Pas d'anes, double-hilt, no knuckle-guard. This is a very unwieldy, point-heavy weapon.
NG	2 lb 14 oz	9 3/4	An inscription on the ricasso indicates that this was made in the castle of Milan as a master-work in 1560. It is an ornately decorated cutting sword with a sharply pointed triangular blade.
60–65	3 lbs 2 oz	10 3/4	Described on object card as perhaps French, c. 1590. The hilt has three rings and knuckle-guard. The blade, despite the exorbitant length, is point-heavy and wants to cut. Despite the rather clumsy weight and balance, A.V.B. Norman opines in a note on the object card that it is genuine, c. 1565–75 (Type 74, according to his typology). A picture of this weapon can be seen in The Academy of the Sword exhibit publication.[3]
50–55	2 lbs 6 oz	9 1/2	Boccia describes this on the object card as northern Italian or French, c. 1570. It is very much balanced for the cut. Broad cutting blade; triple fuller running 1/3 of the length from the hilt; one ring running from pas d'ane to quillion; one counterguard. This is a superb cutting weapon, very "Sainct Didier." A picture can be seen in the Academy of the Sword exhibit publication.
55–70	1 lb 8 oz	10 1/2	Gilt chiseled steel hilt. Very light and well-balanced, with a blade thinning and tapering at the debole.
65–75	2 lb 10 oz	12 1/4	Fine balance and feel to this thrust-oriented weapon. Double-ring hilt with no knuckle-guard; one quillion. La Rocca stated verbally to me that this might be a fake hilt due to the "lifeless" quality of the masks chiseled thereon.

3.   Donald J. La Rocca, *The Academy of the Sword: Illustrated Fencing Books 1500–1800.* (New York: Metropolitan Museum of Art, 1998).

Accession Number	Date/ Provenance	Blade Length	Overall Length (Maximum)	Blade Width	Overall Width (Maximum)	Blade Thickness
12. 14.25.1133	c.1580 Italy	39 3/4	46	1 1/16	10 5/8	3/16
13. 04.03.20	c.1580 Milan (LaRocca speculates the hilt is English.)	39 5/8	45 3/4	7/8	NG	5/16
14. 11.89.1	c.1580 Spanish blade	42 1/4	48 1/8	1 1/4	9 1/8	3/16
15. 29.16.10 "Rapier of Christian I of Saxony."	1580 German (Tarassuk estimates closer to 1600)	38 1/4	46 3/4	1	7	5/16
16. 04.3.32	c.1580–1600	45 1/2	51 1/2	15/16	7 1/8	1/4
17. 40.135.1	c.1590	42 1/2	48 1/2	7/8	NG	5/16

Hardness	Weight	Balance (from Bottom of Pommel)	Remarks
60–70	2 lbs 11 oz	11 1/2	Double-ring hilt with triple counterguard. Despite the broad blade, this is wonderfully balanced for thrusting. Unfortunately, according to notes on the object card, La Rocca, Phyrr, and Boccia all consider it either a composite or entirely fake.
60–70	2 lbs 4 oz	9 3/4	A swept-hilted weapon with a knuckle guard, this has a very nice feel in the hand. The blade is marked CAINO, as is 04.3.32, but, unlike 04.3.32, it is strongly tapered at the debole, making the point extremely responsive.
53–70	2 lbs 10 oz	14	Double-ring hilt, no knuckle-guard, which Phyrr and La Rocca (according to notes on the object card) believe to be associated.
50–65	2 lb 9 oz	12	Rather small two-ring hilt with counterguards; "Ferrara" blade. This is very much a cutting rapier.
70–75	2 lb 13 oz	12 1/2	Boccia claims on the object card that this dates from closer to 1600. Like 04.03.20, the blade is marked CAINO, and is broad, not tapered, at the debole. The weapon is rather point-heavy and unwieldy, possibly due to a re-hilting; the pommel and grip are not original as per object card notes by Boccia and Phyrr.
65–70	2 lbs 13 oz	12	Two-ring hilt, *pas d'anes,* counterguards. Deeply German sculpted, raised crescents on blued steel against a gilt background; straight quillions. The weapon is similar to one shown in the portrait of Matthias, archduke of Austria, c. 1577; however, at least one copy exists. The hexagonal blade is deeply fullered at the forte and stamped IOHA_DECORTA. Though relatively thin and rather long, it is still very much made for the cut, a fact also testified to by the balance of the weapon.

GLOSSARY

This is a glossary of terms and concepts *used in this translation*. Like many other writers of the period, Agrippa often does not use a consistent terminology, but rather describes actions. For clarity, I have frequently used a near equivalent from later fencing terminology; in other cases, I have supplied a more-or-less direct translation of Agrippa's term. The use of such terms within this translation, therefore, does not necessarily match the definitions given by later writers. This glossary is intended to both allow the reader who is familiar with fencing terminology to comprehend the differences in usage and to serve as a reference to both vocabulary and technique for other readers.[1] I have also glossed certain key terms that postdate Agrippa's treatise but aid in understanding his ideas. Where appropriate, I have also given the Italian vocabulary. In no case should this be considered an authoritative guide to early modern fencing technique (insofar as such a thing is possible). Any technical errors are solely my own.

battuta (n), *battere* (v): See **beat**.

beat: A sharp but controlled action against the adversary's blade with the edge of one's own or with the hand or dagger, removing it from the line of attack. (In experiments with reproduction weapons of the type and weight that Agrippa would have used, I have found it most advantageous to beat middle-to-middle.)

capa: See **cape**.

cape: A common outer garment of the sixteenth century, which could also be used to defend against cuts and thrusts when needed.

cartello: A letter, circulated publicly, challenging an adversary to a duel.

cavatione or *cavazione*: The Italian term, postdating Agrippa's treatise, for a **disengagement**.

---

1. See, in particular, William Gaugler, *The Science of Fencing* (Bangor, Maine: Laureate Press, 1997) and *A Dictionary of Universally Used Fencing Terminology* (Bangor, Maine: Laureate Press, 1997); and Jean-Jacques Gillet and Richard Gradkowski, *Foil Technique and Terminology*, 2nd ed. (Staten Island, NY: SKA Swordplay Books, 2000).

close the line: See **line**.

contrapposto: An aesthetic concept of the sixteenth century characterized by a figure putting more weight on one foot than the other, so that the torso rotates around its center. Counterpoise.

contratempo: See **countertime**.

counterattack: An offensive action made against the adversary's offensive action.

countertime: In Agrippa's fencing, to move in the **time** of the adversary's action. (In the modern sense, it is an action made against a counterattack.)

croce: See **cross**.

cross: 1. The **engagement** of the two blades. 2. Defensively, traversely encountering the opposing steel.

dagger: An edged weapon of relatively short length intended primarily for thrusting and, in the case of rapier and dagger fencing, for parrying the adversary's weapon.

debole: The portion of the sword nearest the point, with which one offends the adversary.

deceive: See **disengagement in time**.

disengagement: An action that simultaneously frees one's blade from the adversary's engagement and directs the point so as to threaten him.

disengagement in time: To make an action in response to the adversary's attempt to engage or dominate the blade, so that such contact does not take place and one regains the initiative by threatening the adversary. (In modern fencing terminology, this would be a *cavazione di tempo* (Italian), *derobement* (French).

engagement: (1) The situation of having the blades in contact. (2) The firm yet supple pressure of one blade on another, deviating the opposing point from the **line** of attack.

extraordinary step: See **forced step**.

feint: A feigned attack, made to induce the adversary into disordering himself or moving in a manner that one can take advantage of.

finta: See **feint**.

firma: Literally, "firm"; in context, used to describe a thrust made without moving the rear foot, as in a **forced step**. Leoni (2005) notes that for Fabris' 1606 treatise, this can also mean to make a thrust without moving the feet at all.

forced step: An extra-long step with the front foot used in the attack, thrice as long as the **half-step**. Though clearly the antecedent of the fencing lunge, we have translated this literally so as not to give an anachronistic term.

forte: The portion of the sword nearest the hilt, with the most mechanical advantage, with which one defends oneself.

forza: See **oppose**.

grappling: (1) To make contact on the adversary's body with one's own. (2) Any martial technique that uses such contact to disadvantage the adversary.

guanto di presa: A glove lined with mail, used for parrying or seizing the adversary's blade without harm to oneself.

guard: A position of readiness from which one can attack or defend with equal facility. Agrippa gives four primary guards, numbered "first" through "fourth," and each marked with a letter of the alphabet. He also gives ten other positions derived from these.

hafted weapon: Any weapon consisting of a cutting and/or thrusting head mounted on a wooden pole or haft; a polearm. Agrippa specifically shows halberds.

half-step: One-half of an **ordinary step**.

imbroccata: A descending overhand thrust.

in camisa: Not wearing any defensive armor. Literally "in a shirt."

inside: See **line**.

line: Agrippa speaks of the line in many different ways. The first is the line formed by the body and arm through the weapon, which should usually be as straight as possible (as he shows in Figures 6 and 7). The second is more akin the later use of the term: an imaginary line drawn from the point of the weapon to the intended target. Considered defensively, the adversary's line of attack may be on the outside of one's own sword, that is, to the right of the sword of a right-handed swordsman holding his weapon in a **guard** position, or on the inside, to the left of the sword. (Though Agrippa does not use the term in this way, the line can also be further described as *high* (above the hand) or *low* (below the hand). In the same way, one be said to attack to the adversary's high, low, inside, and/or outside lines. I have used this in the interpretation to clarify some actions.) To *close the line* is to offensively, defensively, or counteroffensively **oppose** the adversary's steel and thus defend oneself.

mandritto, mandritto tondo: A forehand cut (*tondo* simply means "round").

measure: The distance separating two fencers. Simply considered, to be *within measure* is to be able to hit the adversary in a single tempo **(time)**; to be *outside measure* is to be further away than this distance.

measure of the half-sword: The measure at which the two weapons, held in guard, cross middle to middle. This would be considered to be within **measure**.

medesimo tempo: "At the same time." To simultaneously do two things in one tempo **(time)**, such as defending oneself and offending the adversary — for instance, a **countertime** action that deflects the adversary's point to the outside with your *forte* while wounding him (in modern terms, a stop thrust with opposition).

mezzo passo: See **half-step**.

motu propio: In canon law, a decree issued by the pope or a pontifical representative of his own volition, rather than in response to a request. (Literally, Latin for "of its own motion.")

oppose: To control the *debole* of the adversary's blade with the *forte* of one's own in such a way that one protects oneself by closing the **line** in either offense or defense.

ordinary step: To advance the front foot the normal distance on the attack. See **step**.

outside: See **line**, *superficie*.

palma: A unit of measure equal to the span of the four fingers, or about four inches (still in use as the *hand* for measuring horses).

parry: A defensive action of one's own offensive or defensive weapon (or of the unarmed hand) that deviates the oncoming attack.

passo: See **step**.

presa: See **grappling**.

prima: The first **guard**.

provocatione: See **provocation**.

provocation: Any inducement of the adversary to move, whether by feint, false attack, or invitation, so that he can reply and hit.

push: Agrippa's term for making a thrust.

quarta: The fourth **guard**.

riverso: A backhand cut.

Salutiarum: Latin genitive of *Salutiensis* (modern Saluzzo).

seconda: The second **guard**.

second intention: An action undertaken to provoke the adversary into reacting in a manner that one can then take advantage of.

sfalsare: See **deceive**.

sforzare: See **oppose**.

spingere: To **push**.

stance: See **step**.

steccato: A palisade or closed field (cognate with the English *stockade*) within which a formal, legally ordained trial by combat would take place. The use of such arenas, seen in many medieval and early modern fencing treatises, served to create a space where violence could be literally corralled, separated from society at large. To touch the *steccato* meant defeat.

step: Agrippa uses the term *passo* to convey the meanings of both "step" (as in footwork) and "stance" (as in position). Regarding the former, depending on context, Agrippa may speak of using the "step" to advance or retreat, or as part of an offensive action. He prefers the right foot to be always in front, with the feet spaced narrowly (*streta*) or widely (*larga*) depending on circumstances. (For instance, after a **forced step,** one is in a "wide step.")

stramazzone: A vertical downwards cut.

superficie: Literally the "outside of any thing" (Florio) or the circumference of a circle (considering the adversary's body as a sphere). I have translated this as "outside" to avoid confusion.

surface: See *superficie*.

tempo: See **time**.

terza: The third **guard**.

time: (1) A fencing time is the time, relatively considered, that it takes to make one simple fencing action (that is, a single physical motion or action). Though a **half-step**, an extension, and an extension of the arm combined with a **forced step** might be of different durations as measured with a stopwatch, they are all considered to be one fencing time, as they are all single actions. (2) The propitious moment to make an offensive, defensive, or counteroffensive action.

vita: Literally, "waist" or "life," but in Agrippa's usage carrying the connotation of "center of mass."

INDEX

Pages in **boldface** contain illustrations.

This Book Was Completed on September 10, 2009
at Italica Press, New York, New York.
It Was Set in Poliphilus & Bembo
& Printed on 60-lb Natural
Paper in the U.S.A.
and E.U.

Lightning Source UK Ltd.
Milton Keynes UK
UKOW04f1112130214

226402UK00001B/80/P